Seven
in a Jeep

Seven
in a Jeep

A Memoir of the Vietnam War

Ed Gaydos

Columbus Press
P.O. Box 91028
Columbus, OH 43209
www.ColumbusPressBooks.com

EDITOR
Brad Pauquette

PROOFREADER
Mallory Baker

Cover artwork by Dorian Laferre
Design by Brad Pauquette

Print ISBN 978-0-9891737-0-4
Ebook ISBN 978-0-9891737-1-1

Printed in the United States of America
1 3 5 7 9 10 8 6 4 2

Contents

To Kathleen

Forward

I studied seven years to become a Catholic priest. On ordination day, when my classmates lay prostrate before the bishop, I was dodging mortars, ducking sniper fire and shooting howitzers at an artillery firebase in Vietnam.

The firebase sat on a lonely patch of sand in an expanse of rice paddies and meandering streams. It protected the northern approach to Phan Thiet, a supply port on the South China Sea. In a heavy month the firebase shot over 6,400 rounds, more than any artillery battery in central Vietnam they told us. Sometimes it took incoming mortars and rockets two and three times a week, often twice in one night.

We were just kids. Most of us went to Vietnam unwillingly, and we left for war without parades, without fanfare of any kind. We fought, and some of us died, out of devotion to fellow soldiers, not for some larger sustaining cause. Returning home we encountered hostility or worse yet, indifference. What meaning Vietnam had is only what each of us decided it would mean.

I was lucky. After eleven months and a couple close calls,

I returned home with nothing more serious than a skin fungus. I married my sweetheart Kathleen and we had two daughters. After slogging through to a Ph.D. in psychology, I went on to a career with Anheuser-Busch and Limited Brands, retiring a Senior Vice President.

The impetus to write this book came at my sister's wedding in Godfrey, Illinois. My brother Joe and his family were there. His son, not yet a teenager, was anxious to show me a prized possession. Brendon had brought it all the way from San Antonio. In his hands was one of my Vietnam fatigue shirts, folded neatly to reveal its front, like a new shirt in a store. Years ago I had given it to Joe, who wore it for chores around the house. Brendon rescued the shirt and took it into protective custody. As he held the shirt out to me I was shocked to see that the name patch above the right breast pocket was now barely readable. Would this be my legacy, a fatigue shirt with no name, the history it held gone forever and soon to become a rag?

Just a third of us who served in Vietnam are still left. In not many years all 2.7 million of us will be dead, taking to the grave hundreds of millions of untold stories. The website of my old artillery regiment is littered with pleas for information about loved ones who are either dead or frozen in silence about Vietnam.

> *I am looking for anyone that might have served with Spec 5 Michael Ray Atkins from April 1969 to February 1970. I am his wife and he doesn't know I am hunting for anyone. He is fine but don't talk about Vietnam.*

It was time for me to start talking and to leave something

for the next generation beyond dates on a tombstone and an old fatigue shirt.

These are my stories. I made them as close to the facts as I was able by relying on three sources. The first was the stack of letters I wrote to my family and to Kathleen, now my bride of 40 years. I wrote to Kathleen relentlessly from my training assignments and all the way through my tour in Vietnam. I wrote to my family almost as often. God bless Kathleen, my mother, and my younger sister Jayne, who was ten years old when I left for Vietnam. These beautiful women saved every letter.

Two months after arriving in Vietnam I wrote to my parents.

> I didn't intend to yak so much about the war, but I figure you'd rather know exactly what's happening. Some guys tell a lot of happy stories because they figure their folks would worry if told the truth. Others make up a lot of war gore in the hopes that they _will_ worry. The average age in the battery is around 19, and that explains some of it. I'll try to give you something in between, not blood on the paper or bullet holes in the margin.

My second aid was the collection of pictures i took in Vietnam. My camera was a sad little affair, with no light meter and a broken range finder. I took pictures of guys firing howitzers, pulling guard duty and building sandbag bunkers. I took pictures of concertina wire, machine guns, work details, latrines, prostitutes and the aftermath of enemy attacks. The pictures reminded me that most of my fellow soldiers were teenagers, and most of them without high school diplomas. Their pictures, projected large and bright against my study wall, brought them back to life in all their youthful vitality. There they were again, almost life size, mugging for the camera, servicing their weapons, doing their laundry or cleaning up after an attack.

In a final attempt to get the facts right, I spent two days at the National Archives in College Park, Maryland poring through daily staff journals and quarterly reports. The little paragraphs of tightly packed abbreviations played short movies in my imagination—I could almost hear the chop of helicopter blades and the distant echo of machine guns. When I saw numbers labeled KIA and WIA, they came to life as killed or wounded in action, and brought back the chaos and confusion of combat that no report could capture.

I reproduced the dialog in these stories to the best of my memory. Some conversations one never forgets. However, I could not remember the names of four people, so I gave them the names of Rodrigues, Fred, Kline and Delaney. All other names are real—Top, Smoke, Charlie, Curly, Swede, Junk Daddy and the rest. And so are the characters and the dramas we lived together. These are as real to me as yesterday.

Vietnam

*U.S. combat deaths for the month of April, 1970 total
528, bringing the total to 39,328, far exceeding the
number killed in the Korean War.*

In Country

We got our gear at Fort Ord, California: jungle boots, fatigues, blanket, underwear, everything but weapons. Coming in the other direction were guys who looked like they just walked out of the jungle. They were caked in mud and unshaven. They walked with a lethargic shuffle that suggested there wasn't anything anybody could do to them that had not already been done. They laughed at us from across the room. "Hey cherries. Take a look around. Half you guys aren't coming back."

I imagined us moving on conveyor belts running in opposite directions. They were the industrial output of the war. They would be stripped of their soldier's clothing, showered, shaved, repackaged in polo shirts, and recycled back to civilian life. We were the raw material that fed the machine. Half of us who ended up in the field, if you could believe the veterans, would not make it back. But the veterans were wrong about that. I knew the statistics. Then again, you could not believe anything coming out of the Pentagon. Maybe for some units it was true. The guys on the other side of the room were pretty convincing.

I wrote my first letter home on the airplane halfway to

Vietnam.

> I am 35,000 feet above the Pacific just a few hours from Guam. We stopped some hours ago at Hawaii to refuel and stretch our legs. What a beautiful island. Palm trees, flowered sport shirts, and 214 GIs in their jungle fatigues harassing the girls. Our final stop will be at the Philippines before hopping over to Bien Hoa, South Vietnam. It is a 22 hour flight and we have been on the plane for 11 of them. My watch reads 11 o'clock at night. Outside it is broad daylight.

It was night when the plane circled over Bien Hoa, just outside Saigon. Fires dotted the darkness in all directions, like the camps of ancient armies before battle. We were hustled off the plane and onto buses by soldiers in helmets and flak jackets. They all carried M16s. Our destination was Long Binh, a replacement processing facility to the north. As the buses moved through the black, shadows and stray sounds worked on our imaginations. From the back seats someone shouted, "Can't this fucking bus go any faster?"

At Long Binh we fell off the bus into barracks. Later in my first letter from the ground I wrote:

Long Binh is a dirty place. We shared our ramshackle barracks with rats and enormous roaches. At Long Binh I became aware of the peculiar odor of the country. The food had a strange taste.

Daylight revealed a sprawl of plywood buildings with corrugated metal roofs. Crowds of soldiers went about clutching paperwork. No one carried a weapon or wore a helmet. Long Binh turned out to be a small city of clerks, far from the combat zone we had imagined the night before.

Orders came down sending me to the First Field Forces at Nha Trang, 200 miles north, where I would get further orders. This was the beginning of a trickle down process through the seismic layers of military bureaucracy that would eventually result in my final assignment. At each step I had no idea where I would be going next. Even though I had formal training in artillery, nothing said the Army could not make an infantryman out of me, or God-forbid, a cook. I knew only one thing for sure: I was staying in Vietnam.

A C-130 cargo plane waited on the runway to take us to Nha Trang. It had four massive propellers and a wide, drooping belly that almost touched the ground. A ramp led up into its dark rear end, as if the soldiers trooping into it might disappear, and then dissolve, in the lower bowel of a vast military organism. As we boarded, the guy behind me said, "I hear the mechanics who work on these things refuse to ride on them. They have a way of falling out of the sky."

Pallets of boxes and equipment filled the center of the

plane, all of them strapped securely to the floor. We sat in webbed slings, and were strapped with our backs to the outer walls, just so much added cargo. The propellers began to move in slow motion, and as they sped up the plane began to shake. Every part, rivet and bolt took on its own rattle. The plane labored down the runway and by some miracle lifted off the ground. By now the racket was so loud I had to put in my earplugs; it was like riding inside a mechanical bumblebee. Two hours later I stepped off the plane with a buzz in my jaw and feeling like my parts had been mixed up and put back in a different order.

The airbase at Nha Trang was a vast administrative center where the principle mission seemed to be creating paperwork and carrying it between buildings. But unlike Long Binh this was a city lifted whole from the U.S. with all the trappings of home. I marveled at the swimming pools, the movie theaters, the air conditioned buildings. Around every corner there seemed to be another club—this one for officers, that one for sergeants, and yet another for enlisted men, where they all relaxed after long days of toiling over typewriters. No one carried a weapon and it was common knowledge that the base commander had brought his wife over to live with him. On one of my walks around the airbase I fell in with a resident airman. He told me Viet Cong guerillas had attacked the base the previous week. "Rockets," he said.

"Really. How many?"

"One. It hit up there." He pointed to a distant hill I could barely see.

Nha Trang had been a French colonial possession, a seaside resort luxuriating on the South China Sea. The ocean broke to its shore in a ragged white ribbon, and behind it emerald hills rolled to the horizon—foothills and jungle-covered mountains that made up the Central Highlands of Vietnam.

On my walks around the city it seemed to have changed little from colonial times. Palm trees lined avenues of mansions, elegant in pink and yellow stucco. On the beach, fine white sand was a pleasure to bare feet, like walking on sugar.

I spent five days sunning and swimming on the beach. Mama-sans patrolled the beach vending everything from bamboo mats and bananas to marijuana and girls. Everything started at "five dolla" but I soon learned that everything was negotiable, the price would slip quickly to one dollar.

I felt like I was on a five-star vacation, until I received a kind of Vietnam travel brochure to send home. It explained in detail how my family would be notified in the event I was killed or wounded—and warned against malicious hoax calls.

Along with the flyer came my next assignment to the 27th Artillery Regiment, headquartered at Phan Rang further down the coast. Getting there was another Mix Master ride on a C-130, and the airbase was another small American city populated with men in pressed jungle fatigues, each clutching stacks of file folders and hurrying from building to building. Inside the headquarters of the 27th Artillery building I stood at a green metal desk. A clerk with a dead face managed to lift his eyes and say, "Name." He fingered through a stack of papers, found my orders, and handed them to me. "You're going to the 5th Battalion. Be at flight ops at 0700 day after tomorrow...next."

The sun was well up when the plane rattled and shook itself into the air. We were headed for Phan Thiet, a coastal city further south. As we approached the city I twisted in my seat to

SPARE YOUR RELATIVES NEEDLESS GRIEF

Numerous hoax calls to relatives of personnel serving in Vietnam have been reported in recent weeks. These hoax calls have caused considerable anguish and discomfort to the next of kin who are unaware of Department of the Army notification procedures. The hoax calls are malicious and relate primarily to false reports of death, missing, absence without leave, desertion, or other related matters concerning personnel status. The adverse and traumatic impact on the unwary is obvious.

SPARE YOUR RELATIVES THIS GRIEF. Advise them now that they may be the recipient of such a contemptible call, and that any such telephone call concerning your status should be immediately recognized as a hoax.

If your status requires notification of your loved ones, your Army does not use the telephone. Notification is made by a personally delivered message by Army representatives, where identity can be immediately verified; or, by a Western Union telegram which can be verified with the Western Union office from which received; or, by correspondence directly from the Department of the Army. The purpose for notifying your next of kin determines the means used.

look out the tiny window, which gave me only moving snap-shots of the scene below: a river looping through a field of roof tops and slipping into the sea like a giant snake. Fishing boats crowded the water, and along the wharf French colonial build-ings stood shoulder to shoulder with ancient warehouses. The plane banked and revealed a military compound stretched out on a high plateau overlooking the ocean. In a glance I saw sand-bagged buildings, ranks of barbed wire, machine gun towers, and a cluster of artillery pieces. My vacation was about to end.

This was Landing Zone Betty, a sprawling complex that felt a lot bigger on the ground than it looked from the air. I headed out on foot with my duffle bag slung over my shoulder to find my battalion and maybe get orders for my final assign-ment. Nobody was expecting me to show up until the end of the day, so I wandered around the compound with the thought that I would stumble on the 5th Battalion soon enough. Everything was marked with a neat sign, proudly displaying its military unit.

LZ Betty was all about the business of war. Just off the airstrip was a full artillery battery of six guns belonging to A Battery of the 5th Battalion. There was no mistaking the long snout of the 175mm gun, or the wide mouth of the eight-inch howitzer. Walking down the length of the airstrip I passed a dozen assault helicopters of the 192nd . Off the far end of the runway I saw a line of Seahorse transport helicopters, and be-yond them a detachment of the 830th Military Police. I passed an ammo supply bunker for the 1/50 Infantry, then in succes-sion the headquarters of the 3/506 Infantry, a helipad of the 1st Cavalry, a POW camp, fuel storage facilities, and finally the Graves and Registration facility where bodies were identified and prepared for transport home.

I saw no swimming pools or movie theaters, and once off the runway I walked on dirt roads. I had passed from the warm bosom of the Air Force into the hard, calloused hand of the Army. The buildings were flimsy affairs of corrugated metal and plywood, or they were Quonset huts with low half-circle roofs. A few colonial structures with elegant arches remained, their plaster walls now streaked and decaying. The Post Exchange, where soldiers could buy food and clothing, was a small, filthy building with a board leading up to it from the road. Its one civilizing feature was a sign over the door that read, NO LOADED WEAPONS INSIDE. As if in obedience, an armored personnel carrier with a mounted M60 machine gun waited in the street outside. Everywhere clerks and officers in proper uniforms buzzed around administration buildings, while bare chested men in muddy boots leaned in doorways or sat on low sandbag walls smoking and laughing.

The city of Phan Thiet was a short walk up the coast, maybe a mile. I knew that Ho Chi Minh had taught school in Phan Thiet and heard that the locals still sympathized with the Viet Cong, the enemy guerilla force. However on this day I found a peaceful seaside city going about its work-a-day business. Bicycles, motor scooters and rickshaws competed in the streets with military vehicles. Women trotted from the wharf to the market carrying baskets of fish suspended from poles across their shoulders. When a U.S. vehicle passed, hoards of children materialized from the shadows holding out their hands and shouting for handouts. As if on a weekend holiday, South Vietnamese soldiers wearing bush hats and cradling M16s stood in small groups chatting up the local girls. Around mid-afternoon I thought I had better get serious about reporting for duty, and returned to LZ Betty.

Inside the forward command post of the 5th Battalion a clerk behind a metal desk, this one gray, found my orders and told me I was going into the field with Bravo Battery. This battery, he told me, had 105mm howitzers, the smallest and most maneuverable cannon in the Army's arsenal, and was therefore deployed close to the action in direct support of the infantry. Bravo was "air mobile," he added, meaning it sometimes loaded up and went on quick tactical strikes. Right now Bravo Battery was at Landing Zone Sherry somewhere to the north.

Phan Thiet would be my last exposure to running water and all the other small advantages of life in a rear area, even one as primitive as Betty. I planned to spend my last night nursing a couple of cold beers after a long shower, and a battalion clerk stopped by my tent and invited me out to his favorite spot. I grabbed my beers and he rolled a pack of Lucky Strikes into his sleeve. We sat on a hill facing away from town and looked out to the interior of the country. Away from the nighttime glare of airbases, the sky erupted in stars and cast a soft twilight around us, while the valley below receded into an endless black.

The clerk said, "Just so you know, guys back here go through everything shipped to the field. You'll always be short, usually of good stuff like flashlights and poncho liners. And they go through the mail, especially packages. Tell your folks not to send anything valuable."

"That's got to be against some regulation."

He laughed. "Listen to me. Forget your regulation book and any other book you got in your head. This war ain't by the book."

"What then, they just run around doing whatever they want?"

"No. They run around being rear echelon motherfuckers,

or REMF for short."

Pops of light appeared in the dark, like far off flash bulbs. In the time it took to take a breath, sounds of *wump...wump... wump* gave a light tap on my chest. In the distance red tracers shot out in all directions from a dark spot and curved to the ground, looking like legs on a giant spider, pinned to the earth and struggling to move. Flares floated in the sky and lit clouds of drifting smoke.

The clerk said, "Looks like they're getting hit pretty good tonight."

"Wow," was all I could muster.

"That's where you're going tomorrow."

My face went numb and I felt something drop into my stomach. "That's Bravo Battery?"

"Yeah, it gets hit a lot. Don't know why, just seems to be."

An old, neglected thought pushed itself to the surface. *I might die in Vietnam.* "You don't happen to need any more clerks back here do you? I can type."

"I hear that a lot. By the way, what's your favorite shade of purple?"

"Why?"

"We ask guys going to Sherry, 'cause that's the color of the medal most of you come away with."

A Year Earlier

FORT LEONARD WOOD, MISSOURI
BASIC TRAINING

U.S. forces in Vietnam reach a peak of 543,482. The Army opens a formal investigation into the killings of 347 unarmed civilians at the hamlet of My Lai . Three hundred anti-war students at Harvard University seize the administration building.

The Advantage of an Education

The yelling started while we were still on the bus. "Get your asses off this bus…move…move…move." On the tarmac beefy men in uniforms, with strips of scalp showing below their caps, kept up the yelling, filling the air with spit. Duffle bags, knapsacks and suitcases tumbled around us in a litter. The man in charge shouted, "Dump it all out. EVERYTHING. That includes your pockets. And if I see a bulge it better be your dick and not a candy bar from your momma."

The ground became a flea market of socks, underwear, belts, shoes, combs, books, sandwiches, magazines, razors, Brylcreem and the stray condom. The man said, "Put back only what I tell you, nothing more." In loud slow motion he yelled, "One…pair…of…socks."

We all went digging. "You! That piece of monkey shit in the yellow shirt…yes, you…I said ONE."

The drill went on until we had picked out just enough to get us through the next day. The man said, "The rest belongs to Uncle Sam." I left behind a leather-bound copy of *The Origin of Species*, and with it my life as a civilian.

"How many of you are college graduates?" the man asked, now in a friendlier tone. Mine was among half a dozen hands that shot into the air. He smiled and said, "Good, you stay behind. The rest of you uneducated smack heads get in the barracks. Find the bunk with your name and unpack." He turned to us. "I have a special assignment for you college gra–jew–ates." He pointed down the front of the barracks. "Get in a line facing that way."

We shuffled ourselves into a loose line. "Now walk from here to the end of the building. On the way pick up every cigarette butt you see. After I get the babies settled inside I'll be back to inspect. Any butts I find you're going to eat." We made a forlorn little band, stooping for butts and collecting them in careful white piles in the palm of one hand. A soldier watched over us with folded arms.

That night in my bunk I stared at the sag in the springs above my head and marveled at my life. Seven years in a Catholic seminary. A master's degree in philosophy from St. Louis University. Now stripped of possessions and reduced to wondering if the boy above me would wet his bed. How did my life come to this?

The Voice of God

I was fifteen years old when I left home and boarded a bus for St. Joseph's Seminary in Edgerton, Wisconsin. Three of my dad's brothers were Catholic priests and I idolized each of them—one for his intelligence, another for his outgoing personality, and the third for a quiet kindness that seemed to be as natural to him as breathing. I went off to try to be like all of them, and embody their qualities in one perfect priest.

At St. Joe's I made little progress on the road to sainthood. Instead I fell into the rough company of a hundred boys thrown together without mother, father, brother or sister. We slept in massive dorms with the beds arranged in rows, fifty to a room. A row of lockers separated one dorm from the next. We lived out the smallest details of our days in public, with every personal habit and moral failing on display, and therefore subject to ridicule. Nobody escaped. I drew the nickname Gator and felt lucky compared to guys who had to live with Trophy Boy, Cookie Corrigan or Bull Fart. My day was packed with sports, classes, study hall, work details, chapel services and vague exhortations from the adults about the holiness that I could never manage to put into practice. I soon learned to play my small part in the underground market in cigarettes, and sought out the secret places in the utility tunnels that were safe for a smoke. There were clandestine trips into town, secret stashes of money and a vibrant trade in forbidden books. It was all the innocent mischief of a boy's boarding school in the 60s, and I loved it.

After four years at St. Joe's I graduated to the novitiate, a program of spiritual formation at an imposing limestone building near DeSoto, Missouri. Here we began referring to ourselves as monks, and with this my descent continued. In this year of spiritual formation there were no academic classes, only pious reading, meditation, lectures on the religious life, more meditation, chapel services, and finally more meditation until I felt my head would burst.

Most surprising were the practices to discipline the body and remind us of our essential spiritual nature. An arm band made of wire with the ends protruding toward the skin was to be worn every Friday. A small whip made of rope and coated in wax hung in our rooms. Every month we were to kneel in a row outside our doors in a darkened hallway and use the whip on our bare behinds. Wednesday was pill day. We drew small wooden pills from a bag as we entered the dining hall, and on each was a number corresponding to a particular exercise. The most dreaded required the monk to lay across the door of the dining room on the following evening so that the others had to step over his prostrate body. It was dreaded not because of the humility it was designed to engender, but because many stepped directly onto their fellow monk and left gray footprints on the back of his black cassock.

It was hard to take any of this seriously. The prostrate monk would scream in mock agony when someone stepped on him. Most of us in the darkened hallway with our whips in hand beat the wall instead of our butts. And only the most devout continued to wear the wire armband after the first few weeks.

Beyond a silent contempt for these medieval traditions, I fell into open conflict with the novice master over basic Catholic teaching of the time. "You cannot convince me," I said to him before the rest of the monks as we all sat outside after dinner, "that someone is going to hell for all eternity for eating a hamburger on Friday. It is too ridiculous. And this virgin birth thing…" I was fortunate that the fourteen month program ended before he could kick me out.

By a small miracle I still wanted to be a priest after the novitiate, and went on to the next level of education at the major seminary near Oconomowoc, Wisconsin, where I took up studies in philosophy and theology. After the arid months of the novitiate, the seminary at Oconomowoc was like water to a desiccated soul. Our teachers lived in the same building with us and often became companions as much as our professors: the younger priests played on our sports teams, and all were always just down the hall for help on a lesson, or simply to talk. In the classroom they encouraged muscular debate and were uncompromising in their demand for superior work. There were no grades, which paradoxically drove many of us to study deeper and read more widely, to experience the intoxication of learning for itself.

Most of us were from modest backgrounds, and found new worlds opening to us. We could spend the summer with Spanish speaking migrant workers, provided we picked up enough language skills between regular classes. We could volunteer for projects in inner-city Detroit, where the nights were filled with sirens and the occasional gunshot.

The seminary building sat on gorgeous Lake Oconomowoc, so big you could not see across it. In winter we ice skated and sailed iceboats. During the summer we fished, swam and took long sailboat rides. Friendships grew deeper by the year, the kind that last a lifetime. Why would anyone want to leave such a life?

The Matthys sisters, Rosie and Dianne, were regular visitors to the seminary. They came every few months to see their two brothers. The girls went about surrounded by a phalanx of grinning monks. I never had the courage to talk to either one of them. Instead I suffered from afar. I was in the chapel attending mass when a wave of perfume washed over me. I looked up to see the Matthys girls two pews in front of me. My stomach ached and I sat in a twist of fear and bliss that no prayer could unravel. A voice from somewhere said: *Frater Gaydos, you need to find another line of work.*

I was twenty-two years old when I walked out the front door of the seminary with a trunk containing all my possessions and $50 in my pocket. At the end of a lonely train ride back to St. Louis I moved to my parents' basement, into a tiny bedroom my dad had walled off beside the furnace. I had no plan, no direction in life. For want of anything better to do I enrolled in a Master's program in philosophy at St. Louis University. To support myself I worked the night shift in a department store warehouse just down from the university. By day I studied the epistemology of David Hume, I untangled the categorical imperatives of Immanuel Kant, and I labored to understand Thomas Aquinas in the original Latin. Then I walked to my warehouse job beneath the viaduct on South Grand Avenue. There I got a different kind of education. I watched the professors of thievery sneak televisions past the security guard. I saw them wear old shoes into the building and walk out in new ones.

The Vietnam draft was in full swing, and protests against the war were in full flower. Every few days one of my classmates announced, "My trunk is packed, baby, and I'm headed for Toronto." I had no strong feelings against the war, and not enough guts to leave the country. So I waited. Every Monday morning I called my draft board and asked if my notice would be going out. The lottery did not yet exist and they were taking the oldest first. At twenty-five I was ripe for the picking.

In the meantime I failed at every effort for a spot in the reserves. So I worked to get into the Air Force, which seemed like a safe place to ride out the war. A department head at the Air Force Academy said there was a good chance he could get me on the teaching staff if I got my Master's and became an officer. Off I went in high hopes to the Air Force recruiting office near the university.

"You're a shoo-in for officer training," the recruiter said.

I took the required tests and to my surprise qualified for pilot training. The recruiter wanted me to take the physical, even though I needed glasses to see past the front of my car.

"Who knows," he said, "you might pass."

"No," I said, "I'll be a line officer and then try for the Academy."

"OK, but keep checking with your draft board, and before your notice goes out come on back and we'll get you signed up."

One morning the draft board lady, who sounded like a grandmother, said, "It's going out this week, honey."

Down to the Air Force office I went ready to sign up, only to learn that all the officer training slots were filled. The recruiter said, "But you should enlist as an airman—it's only for four years—and then apply for officer training again in a year or so."

I knew he had lied to me and said to him, "I am not spending four years scrubbing runways."

Now I was only days, maybe minutes, away from a "Greetings" letter, and in a mild panic. If I got drafted I would end up carrying a rifle through some Vietnamese jungle, and sure to come back in a box. I headed for the Army recruiting office just a few doors away to see what options I had before my notice went out. I explained what had happened with the Air Force. "You sign up right now," the recruiter said, "and we'll put you in officer training. Of course you got to pass the test."

"I passed the Air Force test."

"Then you'll be fine. And hey, we let you pick your specialty. Keep you out of the infantry if you want."

"Yes, I want."

"There's also this little deal called a deferral. You don't have to show up for six months from today."

That cinched the deal. Six months would give me time to finish my Master's. And who knew, maybe the war would end. I committed to the standard two year enlistment, plus another ten months for being an officer. On the form I had to check a box for what specialty I wanted. There were four listed, and I picked combat engineering. I had no idea what a combat engineer did, but it seemed more glamorous and probably safer than infantry, artillery or tanks.

My life in the Army began with the physical, even though I was months away from wearing a uniform. The physicals were at the Mart Building on the southern edge of downtown St. Louis. The Mart was constructed in the depth of the depression in 1931 without a hint of architectural adornment. It was a limestone giant, looking down with row upon row of windows, vacant eyes without eyebrows. The entire ninth floor was devoted to physicals.

I joined a roomful of guys seated on gray plastic chairs. A soldier entered carrying a clipboard. He announced, "If you're here for the Navy, pay attention. The following individuals come with me." He read off four names, and as the young men stood up, the soldier said, "You guys are going to be Marines." Without objection they followed him from the room, like cattle to the knife.

The fellow seated next to me leaned in, "Can they do that?"

"I think they just did," I said. "Welcome to the military."

Soon another soldier came and called my name along with six others. In the changing room we stripped down to our shoes and underpants. We stayed this way for the entire day, carrying our valuables in brown paper bags. We went from station to station, guided by a network of colored lines on the floor. Each color led to its own indignity. At the end of the red line we dropped our shorts and coughed. The green line directed us to the place where we bent over and relaxed.

At the end of the brown line we picked up sample cups and took up positions along a row of urinals. The guy to my right was having some difficulty, as often happens to boys trying to perform in public. He tapped the shoulder of the fellow next to him, "Do you mind?" He moved the cup down to his new friend and took a sample. Military teamwork.

We paraded along the colored lines. At times we encountered other groups coming in the opposite direction or intersecting at corners. It was a beehive of half-naked bodies of all shapes, in underwear of all variety and color, everyone clasping brown bags to their navels and trying not to lose the line of march. I was in my tighty-whities and wishing I were a boxer man. Lunch was at the end of the blue line. The brown bags sat beside plates or balanced on laps. Viewed across the tabletops the room could have been the cafeteria at a nudist colony.

It was rush hour when I caught the bus for home that evening. I wedged myself into the standing crowd and felt like I had on too many clothes.

The Joy of Basic

The first morning of basic training we lost our hair. The barber took a glutton's delight in every head that came into his chair, smiling and licking a lower lip. He loved hippie hair, the long waving locks and the halo-sized afro. With a turn of the wrist he placed the clippers at the hairline between the eyes, then worked a slow, sensuous stroke straight over the top and down to the nape of the neck, making a clean road with hemispheres of jungle on either side. We whistled and cheered our approval as the barber cleared the rest of the head in quick strokes. Soon we all stood with naked knobs—real U.S. Army dickheads.

That afternoon we surrendered our civilian clothes, the last shreds of civilian life. We filed into a large room where bins of military clothing lined the walls. At each bin a supply clerk took a glance at each of us. Reaching behind without looking he pulled hats, boots, fatigue shirts, trousers, socks and boxer drawers. We carried the piles to the next room where we stripped out of our civvies and pulled on our uniforms. Some of them fit. When I put on my boots I felt a stab of pain in my

24

right foot. The insole was curled at the edge and it felt like I was walking barefoot on a twig.

I complained to the sergeant, "My foot is killing me."

He was unmoved. "You'll get used to it."

"I don't think so."

He came out with something I would hear a lot in the Army, "Sounds like a personal problem, soldier."

We rose before dawn for calisthenics, grunting out jumping jacks in front of the barracks. We ran everywhere. We cleaned boots and stood for inspection. We practiced *left face* all morning, then *right face* all afternoon. We dropped for twenty pushups outside the mess hall and polished whatever did not move. We took showers in a room lined with shower heads, a drain in the middle of the floor. We sat on commodes along the wall an arm's length apart, chatting and passing the toilet paper. We slept three feet from one another, stacked two high in bunk beds. We ate elbow to elbow. We yawned, burped and farted with impunity. We bragged about fictional sex lives.

The Army was a lot like the seminary. Except in the seminary we did not talk about sex, we just thought about it a lot.

Conversations with a drill sergeant came down to standing at attention while he yelled two inches from the trainee's face. A young black drill sergeant off the streets of Detroit called me aside after I had taken a yelling from a fat sergeant. "Listen man, you are taking this too serious. You looked about to cry."

"I was not crying, Drill Sergeant."

"I know, relax. You just looked it."

"I was not about to either…Drill…Sergeant." I was mad.

"Take it easy, Private, I'm on your side. Here, try this. Look at me." He stared into my face with a faraway look. "Know what I'm doing? Look close. Can you tell?"

"I can see you got a dumb look on your face, no offense, Drill Sergeant."

"You got it. A dumb look. Know how I got this dumb look?"

"From your mother?"

"Another crack about my mother and I'll make you really cry, hear me?" He relaxed into his childhood dialect. "You be callin' for your own momma. Now I don't wanna bother with you." He put his arm in the air and started to walk away.

"Please, Drill Sergeant, I'm sorry. It just came out."

He turned around and faced me. "So here's the look I give to dumb shits like you making dumb shit sounds out of your shit filled mouth. I give you the look. Like this." His face went blank, his eyes again far off. "So what am I doing, what am I doing?"

"Seems like you're looking at something behind me."

"Yes. I am looking right through your empty skull. Think you can do that? Do it the next time one of these white mothers gets in your face. It'll drive'm nuts," he walked off waving his arm again. "Still don't know why I bother with you."

Garza

Training was mostly outdoors. It seemed to rain every day, by order of the Army I suspected. We had ponchos, but had to wait for permission to put them on, which came only after we were thoroughly soaked. We lived in soggy boots. We crawled in the mud. We stood shivering for eternities in long lines outside the mess hall. I cannot remember a time not being cold, hungry and exhausted. The barracks at night echoed with coughing, hacking, wheezing, sniffling and labored breathing. Our sergeant told us that being in the Army meant living with a constant cold. "So get used to it," he said.

One morning I could barely breath, and my chest made a funny sound. At the infirmary the doctor told me to take off my shirt. He looked closely at my back. "You've got the measles. It's going around the base."

I said, "Sir, that's impossible, I already had the measles."

He gave me the first kind look I had received in the Army. "Son, you have the measles and I am admitting you to the hospital." I sank into a warm, dry bed in a room filled to the corners with…silence. Blessed silence. Then blessed, blessed sleep.

27

The first morning on the measles ward I learned none of us had the measles. We all had upper respiratory infections, standard issue URI.

Every morning our nurse lined us up in the hallway in our hospital gowns for inspection. She was a bantamweight and beef jerky tough. Before starting on her inspection she said, "I don't want to see any salutes from below the belt." She walked the length of our formation, stopped in front of each man and looked him up and down. On occasion she smiled, but never gave a sign of what she was looking for. When she stopped in front of me the first morning I could look down on the top of her head and see her scalp. She lifted her gaze and gave me an appraising look. God forgive me and the saints deliver me, I found her alluring. If she made any unscheduled house calls during the night I was not aware of them, nor did I hear any stories going around the ward. One could only wait and hope.

I was in the hospital five days and returned to training feeling fit. When I reported to the sergeant he said, "You've been recycled."

"What's that?" I knew the answer could not be good.

"It means you have to start basic from the beginning."

My bowels sank to my boots. "But why, Sergeant? I'm feeling great."

He flipped open a file. "Let's see. It says here you missed a portion of dismounted drill."

"I was only gone five days. Sergeant, I had *left face* and *right face* down cold."

"This last week was *about face*, *column left* and *column right*. The Army thinks you need to go back and pick that up… in a new trainee class."

"That's ridiculous, Sergeant."

28

"Yeah, probably."

The barracks in my new unit was a World War II Quonset hut, a half-circle building made of corrugated metal. It looked like a drainage tunnel with a door. A clerk showed me to my spot at the end of the row. "Here's you," he said.

It was an empty space. I said, "Where's my bunk?"

"You don't have one," he said and walked out.

Later that day I met Garza. He was on my immediate left in formation because we lined up alphabetically. Garza was from New Jersey. He had a bucktooth smile and calculating eyes that said he had the Army figured out. He said the next barracks over was vacant and we should trot over there and grab a bed. We strode down the aisle of the unoccupied barracks shopping for a bed. A door at the far end of the building opened, revealing a figure in silhouette against the bright background. He yelled at us, "You soldiers, come here." We walked to him. "What are you soldiers doing in here? You're not authorized to be in this building."

"I needed a bed and…"

Garza cut me off, "Just looking around, Sergeant."

"No, you were stealing government property."

We marched behind him to his company commander's office, and from there got handed over to our own company commander. We were charged with leaving our unit compound, unauthorized entry and attempted theft. The neighboring unit had experienced some missing equipment and they needed to hang someone. Garza and I would do. We got Article 15s, non-judicial punishments that saved the Army the trouble of a court martial.

We were confined to the company area for two weeks, could not have weekend passes for the rest of the training cycle, and had to give up a week's pay, which came to $22.50. The Article 15s would be a part of our personnel records for one year.

Before long our two weeks were up. Finally outside of our dog pen, Garza and I were walking beside a water tower when he said, "Hey, let's climb that thing and see what the view is like." Ft. Leonard Wood sat in the center of the Mark Twain National Forest, the foothills of the Ozark Mountains. From the top of the tower we looked out over hills ordered row upon row to the horizon. They were winter gray, but brushed with the first green of spring. Garza leaned over the rail and spat. The gob curved in the breeze, broke into pieces and disappeared under the tower. He said, "Let's go on the other side and piss with the wind. I'll bet we can hit the captain's roof."

On our way down from the tower, just as we were stepping off the last rung, a voice from around the corner said, "You soldiers, come here." Garza and I looked at each other and shook our heads. We clamped a hand over our name patches and took off at a dead run. We were not about to make the same mistake again.

Looking casual we returned to the barracks from the opposite direction of the water tower. That evening a lieutenant appeared at our formation. He was looking for two soldiers from our unit he had seen on his tower and who had disobeyed a direct order. He was a new second lieutenant, and still touchy about his image. The company stood at attention as he walked up and down the ranks. Garza and I stood side by side in the second row, two culprits gift wrapped for the taking. The lieutenant looked each man in the face as he walked along the first row. When he turned the corner and started down our row, I felt Garza's elbow and heard a low snort. He was having fun. I was petrified. The lieutenant looked at us and inspected our

30

name patches, first GARZA then GAYDOS. Without a trace of recognition he moved on.

From that day I kept my distance from Garza. I could not afford to lose another $22.50.

The Bully

He slept two bunks down on my left. On the inside lid of his footlocker he kept pictures of two older brothers serving in Vietnam. One was a Marine and the other an infantry rifleman. He looked forward to joining them in the holy work of "wasting gooks." At bayonet training he made runs at the dummy with a demon scream and attacked with a frenzy that surprised even the drill sergeant. He plunged the bayonet into its bowels with a blood lust: once, twice, a third time with a twist.

He was thick about the neck and shoulders, with bullet-hole eyes. In casual conversation he said to me, "I could probably kill you right now with my bare hands if I wanted to. My brother, he's a Marine in Vietnam, he showed me how. Maybe I'll do it while you're asleep tonight." He spoke with his hands in fists and his elbows out.

I know why he picked me for this little display. I was skinny, so thin as a child I wore two undershirts to school to add a little bulk to my frame. At bayonet training I was the despair of the drill sergeant. I could not get the yell right. My "YAAAAAAA" was not enough to scare a butterfly off a petunia. The drill sergeant got into my left ear and screamed, "Private, you are not mad enough. Do it again." Off I went on a second and then a third run. I could feel the looks of the other trainees. The drill sergeant shook his head and waved me on, another momma's boy.

Late one night, through the coughing and rattled breathing, I heard a faint noise coming from his bunk. It was the sound of muffled weeping, him crying into his pillow. We all heard it, but nobody wanted to get into another guy's personal life, so we said nothing. Even if we had wanted to help, we did not have the language for it. The only words we had were *nuts, crazy* or the military catchall of *personal problem*. When it came to the interior life, we all suffered alone and in silence, like marbles in a bag touching no deeper than the surface.

I heard him crying often, sometimes a short whimper and sometimes for almost half an hour until he fell asleep. I took comfort that when he was busy crying he probably wouldn't think to kill me that night.

You Bet Your Ass

Midway through basic we got our rifles. The M14 weighed almost twelve pounds with a fully loaded magazine. Even though it was being replaced in Vietnam by the lighter M16, it still served as the standard issue rifle for basic training.

The drill sergeants waxed poetic in describing the close relationship between a soldier and his rifle. It was to be our girlfriend: handled with love, oiled with care, fired with orgasmic ecstasy and cleaned with post-coital tenderness. It was the first thing the Army said that made any sense. We tore down, cleaned and reassembled our rifles so many times that in a final exercise we performed the task blindfolded. "If you can't do it in the dark," the drill sergeant said, "you don't deserve her."

God help the recruit who called it a gun. The drill sergeant made him stand in front of the formation with one hand holding his M14 and the other on his crotch. He was made to shout for all to hear, "This is my rifle, this is my gun. One is for shooting, the other's for fun." It was a mistake nobody made more than once.

A special trainee in my platoon carried a broomstick in-

34

stead of a rifle. He had declared himself a conscientious objector and was to become a medic. He shouldered his broomstick with as much pride as we our rifles. He marched, ran and crawled in the mud with the rest of us. The drill sergeants, normally ready with insults for any occasion, called him Private Jones—when we were shitheads, pussies and smack heads. They said "please" to him. They treated him as a man with the strength of his convictions and the courage to serve on the front lines of combat. They saw the rest of us as candy-asses who would rather be somewhere else, and they were right.

Every day we marched three miles to the rifle range with thirty pounds of gear and our beloved rifles. By this time the insole in my boot had found its proper place. Part of the way we double-timed, a kind of half-run. The guys with loose packs left a trail of tinkling forks and spoons on the road. One poor soul lost his entire mess kit. It rolled along the road and then off into the ditch like a lost hubcap. When he broke from the formation to retrieve it, the sergeant grabbed him by his pack and hauled him back into line. "No you can't go back and get it," the sergeant yelled. "You'll eat with your fingers."

Toward the end of a long double-time run the trainee in front of me drifted sideways, wobbled and went down in a heap. The column of soldiers flowed around him like a stream around a dead moose. The next day we saw him with nasty scratches along the side of his face. After that the guys who fainted on long marches always landed on grassy spots along the side of the road. I could see them picking out their spots. That lasted two days. Anyone fainting on grass would find the drill sergeant screaming him back onto his feet and cursing him back into line. A fainting trainee had to go face first into the asphalt or he was faking.

35

On long marches we chanted:

> *We like it here*
> *We like it here*
> *You bet your ass we like it here.*

A Tale of Two Drill Sergeants

The fat one said to us "Boys, there's two rules for getting by in the Army. The more you know the less you work, and never walk when you can ride." The most walking he ever did was out to his jeep, where he wedged his stomach behind the wheel and said, "OK boys, let's go." He rolled along with us on long marches promising the whole way, "It's just around the next bend." He brought a .22 rifle with him, and when we were at the firing range or on bivouac he went off and shot squirrels from his jeep.

The other drill sergeant could have stepped off a recruiting poster. His Smokey-the-Bear hat sat on his head at a forward tilt, giving his body the look of an animal about to pounce. He ran everywhere his troops ran. He said, "The day I can't outrun you marshmallows is the day I retire." Like drill sergeants through the centuries he pretended to be deaf. "I CAN'T HEEEEAR YOU."

"YES, DRILL SERGEANT," we responded in a tonsil tearing roar.

When Drill Sergeant got us up at 5:00 in the morning for

calisthenics, bleary eyed and stumbling from the barracks, he was already dressed "tight" and looked like he had never been to bed. He led us on six-mile marches to the firing range and back. He went with us on bivouacs and surprised us in the middle of the night with forced marches in full gear and gas masks. Drill Sergeant was the first real man many trainees had ever met, and the first to push them to be men themselves.

By the final week of training our unit had hardened to the outdoor life. Our M14s were no longer heavy hunks of wood and iron, but our closest friends and now somehow lighter. Some guys had lost twenty pounds. One trainee who could only hang under the chin up bar and wiggle on his first day could now snap off ten. On long marches we chanted cadence so the next county could hear us. That earned us the right to march with musical instruments. One soldier got a trumpet from home, others got a snare drum and a trombone. Our song was "Sweet Georgia Brown," which we fired up when passing neighboring units to excite their envy. We were becoming a cohesive military unit. Only one test remained. Crawling under live machine gun fire.

We assembled at the firing range at midnight. It had been raining all day, and floodlights cut through the mist. A blanket of barbed wire, held up by stakes, covered the field. At the far left, gray and menacing, was the machine gun emplacement. Our mission was to get across the field.

Drill Sergeant gave us final instructions. "Number one, don't lose your rifle. You come across without it and you will go back and get it, even if it takes you all night and you come back with an ass full of lead." We stared at the machine gun. "Number two, don't stand up. That .50 caliber over there is firing live ammo. For those of you who need it simple, the bullets are real and they are four feet in the air. You will not panic. You may piss in your pants, you may vomit your miserable guts out, you may dig a tunnel with your dick—I don't care—but you will not stand up. Any questions?"

A voice came from the crowd. "What would happen, Drill Sergeant?"

"You go home in box A and box B."

Lizard-like we slipped into the muck under the first line of barbed wire, rifles cradled across our arms. I pulled forward with my knees and elbows, trying to keep my rifle dry. The world above exploded and pushed my chin into the mud. I heard bullets just over my back like little freight trains. I had fired the .50 caliber on the practice range, but I was not prepared for the racket on the other end, the business end. I inched forward. Midway across the field and by now used to the noise, I turned on my back to get a better look. I saw a river of red tracers flowing above me. For every tracer there were four more bullets, all tearing above me like a single mechanical beast. I lay still. I wanted to reach up and touch it. I wondered if anyone had stood up? It did not matter, because I knew the bullets were higher than advertised. The Army was not about to let some crazy kid get killed.

Looking around I saw that I was alone in the field. Back on my stomach I put my butt in the air and scrabbled forward. Drill Sergeant was counting noses as I passed under the last of the barbed wire. "Nice of you to join us," he said.

The Art of Promotion

After the adventure with Garza I changed my ways, determined to recover from the Article 15. I was not meant for a life of crime. I aced the tests on military protocol, easy by just reading the material. I paid attention to my uniform. At inspection my gig line was always perfect: shirt edge, belt buckle and pant fly all in alignment. I swiped the all-important belt buckle with a shirtsleeve one last time before coming to attention, guaranteeing against the stray fingerprint. I melted the polish on my boots with a lighter to make them look like patent leather. When Drill Sergeant inspected my rifle and looked down the barrel, he never saw a hint of rust. I made my bunk so tight the edges of the mattress curved upward. I always kept my locker in order for snap inspections. At the firing range I qualified at the highest level of expert, and I never flagged on marches or in physical training. I helped the other trainees, and maybe because of my age I became an older brother to some of them. Above all I was careful in my dealings with Garza.

Shortly before graduation I received a formal letter from the dean at St. Louis University regarding the granting of my

Master's degree. It stated that if I did not attend the graduation ceremony I would not get my degree. The graduation date was the same day as graduation from basic training. I wrote back:

> Dear Dean,
>
> I would be delighted to attend the graduation ceremony for the formal granting of my degree. However, at the moment I have another commitment. I am in Army basic training at Ft. Leonard Wood, Missouri. Would you please write to my commanding officer requesting my presence on that day? Below is his contact information.

The diploma arrived in the mail three weeks later.

Graduation from basic took place on a glorious day in late May. The breeze brought a smell of new leaves off the Ozark hills. The stands were filled with officers, sergeants, dignitaries and visitors. Battalions, companies and platoons marched in military cohesion past the stands, while a band played in cadence to the waves of moving legs. As units passed the post commander, heads turned to face him and arms rose in salute. Unit flags recalled campaigns in North Africa, France, Italy, Korea and Vietnam. Then the ghosts showed up, seeming to march in formation behind the waving colors. My father appeared, who served on a sub chaser in the North Atlantic during WWII. His brother Johnny Joe came next. Johnny Joe enlisted in the Marines right after Pearl Harbor and died a few months later on Tulagi at the battle of Guadalcanal. Next came uncles Scott and Phil, who served in that same Great War.

At the ceremony I was named trainee of the cycle for my company. The battalion colonel read from the award citation.

> *You have exhibited the highest degree of proficiency, devotion to duty, and sense of discipline. As a result of your exemplary performance, you have been selected as the outstanding trainee of your company during cycle two. You show potential for future leadership positions with added responsibilities.*

I began as a recycled, Article 15 screw-up and somehow managed to redeem myself. Up to this telling it has been one of my secret prides. But the Army never let you feel good for long. At graduation promotions to E-2 went to the top third of the class, giving them a single stripe on their sleeves. I did not get a stripe, probably due to my Article 15. Army logic concluded that the number one trainee did not necessarily have to be in the top third of his class.

I noticed that a promotion went to the biggest clown in the unit, a kid who barely got through the day. I asked him later how that happened. He said, "A couple weeks ago I was walking through the office delivering something to the captain. There wasn't anybody around. The place was like empty. I saw this paper on the desk with a bunch of names circled. It was the promotion list. I just picked up the pen that was laying there and circled my name. Pretty cool, huh?"

I thought, *Let him have his promotion. He'll probably never see another. Then again, he might end up a general.*

The company commander told me to carry my personnel records to my next assignment. I had been recycled, so the records did not travel in their normal channels.

"Don't open the file," he said.

"Yes, sir." Around the first corner the Article 15 found its way into my pocket.

Four-Star Private

I was in a dangerous spot, a trainee without a job. Until my new orders were issued the Army had to figure out what to do with me. There was always a need to paint rocks. The Army's way of sprucing up the neighborhood was to line walkways with white rocks. I had seen battalions of soldiers bending over with paintbrushes and buckets, and figured that was not for me. I asked to see the company commander. "Sir, I was wondering if I could work around the office. I can type and I'm good at it."

He looked me over, flipped through my file and told me to come back in the morning. "Report to the corporal," he said.

The corporal was a teenager and trouble from the beginning. He swaggered around the office when the officers were gone and worked his authority over me in arbitrary and demeaning ways. He mocked my education. He ridiculed my age. He ordered me to re-do work that was done well the first time. On the fourth day when we were alone, he came at me again. I reached out and fingered the stripes on his arm. I said, "If it weren't for these I would kick your skinny ass." I had only

44

been in one fight my entire life. In grade school I got whipped by a kid half my size. But I was a head taller than the corporal, six years older, and in good shape despite looking like a beanpole. Most of all I was a good actor. Thank God he bought it and never bothered me again. I soon worked my way into the captain's good graces, making the corporal irrelevant. I had that one advantage. I could type.

Typing was not a trivial skill in 1969. Underwood typewriters were substantial hunks of metal, about the weight of a bowling ball. The keys were flat discs arranged in tiers, like bleacher seats at the ballpark. To do their job they needed a blow straight down in the center, requiring the hands to move around a great deal to reach all the keys. Hitting a key would leverage up a thin metal arm toward the roller, striking an ink ribbon positioned in front of the paper. When an errant finger struck two keys at once, the arms scissored together in a tight embrace as they came racing upward. Usually they locked halfway up. If they managed to reach the roller they made two half letters, or one would win the race and make a single weak image.

Military paperwork required an original and two carbon copies. That meant there were five pieces of paper in the typewriter: three white and two carbon sheets. It took mean, wicked strength to strike the keys with enough force to get the carbons to take. An hour of pounding made my forearms ache. Correcting a typo was a minor project. The papers had to be removed, the typo rubbed out with a good eraser on all three copies, then the papers and carbons put back in their exact prior position. Because the ink on the carbon at the mistake had already been used, the clerk had to strike the proper key with a mighty whack. A cleanly typed document was a thing of beauty. Officers put great stock in the good impression it created with their superiors, making an officer and his clerk brothers in arms.

Company clerks spent most of their time typing Article 15s, three pages of legal size paper, single-spaced. I was midway through the paperwork on a sergeant who pushed a trainee down a flight of steps when the perpetrator walked into the office. He was from my previous unit and must have been tipped off to the work on his Article 15. He walked to my desk holding his hat in front of him. He paused and I thought he was going to genuflect. "Good to see you again, Private. Can I talk to you for a minute?" He got right to the point, "I see you're working on my stuff. I want you to know I didn't push him on purpose. I can't get another Article 15, it'll be my third this year." Only days before he was kicking my trainee behind, and now he was kissing it.

"Sergeant, I'll do what I can," I lied. Here was a new power and it made me feel a little drunk.

The captain signed weekend passes, but Company Clerk Gaydos controlled them. He acted as gatekeeper into the captain's office. He said who could see the captain, or in what order. He decided if the captain was in or out. He arranged the papers for the captain to sign. Some he put on top of the stack, some he forgot in the drawer and on some he had an opinion. Lieutenants, sergeants, corporals, specialists and privates came to his desk with their requests. He gave the same reply to everybody, "I'll do what I can." The logic was simple. For them there was nothing to lose and a lot to gain from puckering up. For the clerk there was nothing to gain by saying no, and a lot to gain from saying maybe.

Army uniforms were like billboards. Patches, pins, medals and insignia advertised everything worth knowing—rank, specialty, combat campaigns, past assignments and performance in the field. It took only a second to read the uniform of a captain with two Vietnam service ribbons, a Purple Heart and a Silver Star. The salute to him had to be a good one. My uniform was as naked as the day it came from the factory, with the exception of my name patch. I was still an E1, a rank so low it did not merit even a single stripe on the sleeve. On my walks around the post, the officers returned my salutes with limp, halfhearted waves at their foreheads. But inside the company compound I got salutes from first and second lieutenants they would give a four-star general.

I came and went as the job let me. I did not bother to tell the officer in charge where I would be or when I would return. I gave myself two hours for lunch and went swimming at the post pool. I shopped at the Post Exchange. I worked on my tan. If you could type you could get away with anything.

A Preview of Vietnam

A new first lieutenant showed up, just back from Vietnam. He had sandy hair and a little boy's freckled face. Under the glass on his desk he kept Polaroid pictures of dead Viet Cong. "There was more," he said, "but there wasn't always a camera. See, we'd scare them into the brush—you know, kind of surround them like, get them to where they weren't moving." A light came into his eyes. "We'd chew the holy bejesus out of them bushes. Then we'd go looking for bodies. Drag them out and, you know, line them up, like hunting deer, because we had to count them. Them fellas in the rear was on us all the time for a number, and hell, maybe there was three on the grass but we said six. Always figured maybe we missed a few."

I would be in Vietnam in a few months. Lord help me. I went to see the captain, hoping to keep my clerk job.

"Private, I'd love to keep you," he said. "But you're slated for Officer Candidacy School. Engineers, right? At Fort Belvoir in Virginia. OCS orders are cut out of Washington. I can't touch you."

48

FORT SILL, OKLAHOMA

Secretary of State Henry Kissinger conducts his first secret meeting in Paris with representatives from Hanoi. The Viet Cong begin a new offensive attacking 150 targets throughout South Vietnam. Ho Chi Minh dies of a heart attack the following month at the age of seventy-nine. In his will he urges the North Vietnamese to fight on "until the last Yankee is gone."

The Communist

I did not go straight to Fort Belvoir. The next rung on the ladder to becoming an officer was Advanced Individual Training at Fort Sill, Oklahoma. It was a special program for guys going to OCS. We were all college graduates, victims of a draft that was taking the oldest first.

The first morning we herded into a large room with rows of folding chairs. Sergeant Rodrigues went to the front, raised his chin and yelled, "Anybody play baz—a—ball? College, minors, triple A?"

I put up a hand. "How about basketball?"

"No. Baz—a—ball." Then louder and slower. "BAZ—A—BALL . You make the team of the general, maybe you stay here."

Me and baseball. Not a chance.

One afternoon Sergeant Rodrigues said to me, "Tomorrow you teach the class."

"Me, Sergeant?"

"You teach. Tomorrow."

"Sergeant, on what?"

50

He gave a one word answer, the first syllable a small explosion, "COM-munism."

"What am I supposed to say?"

He put a finger in the air. "Communism. One hour. You teach." Then he was gone.

All I knew about communism was what I had learned in school about Karl Marx. It probably was not what the Army had in mind, but it was all I had. The next morning I stood in front of the class while Sergeant Rodrigues paced the back of the room.

I opened with, "This class is on communism." I looked out on blank faces, all about to take a nap. I decided to have a little fun. "All of you are nothing. You're big fat zeros. Me too, I'm a zero." I drew a circle in the air with my arm. Twice. A few heads came up. "We're all nothing without other people. You can't be a son without parents. You can't be a husband without a wife. Or a brother without a sibling. You can't be a soldier without other guys in the army like you. You can't be anything without other people. Think about it for a minute and you can't come up with a single thing you are all on your own. And look at the clothes you have on, the car you drive. You wouldn't have any of that if there was just you trying to make stuff. OK, so what? I'll tell you so what. Here is where the communism thing comes in. All of us are more important than some of us. Communism says we have to worry about what's good for everybody, not just what's good for a few. It gets better. The people who work—like in factories and even offices—should get the most from what they do instead of all the money going to a rich boss or some company. Think about it. It's just not fair when the people who do all the work end up on the short end of the stick. People get really mad when the fat bosses end up with

51

all the money and never get their hands dirty. Pretty soon they figure out the only way to make things right is to get out their guns and start shooting."

I saw Sergeant Rodrigues pacing faster, a dark look on his face. "The communists think that's going to happen here. We have capitalism and think anybody should be able to make as much money as they can and there shouldn't be any rules to get in the way. You can walk over anybody you want, just to make a buck. We make heroes out of millionaires. Everybody wants to be like Andrew Carnegie. But the way it works out there's only one Carnegie, and everybody else ends up working in his steel mills. And let me tell you something about Mr. Andrew Carnegie, the richest man in America back then. He cut the wages of his workers twenty percent because he could get away with it. A couple years later he closed the mill ten days before Christmas. And when 1,600 workers and their families were freezing and starving and had no money to buy coal, he opened the mill and cut their wages another third. The communists have a fancy way of saying it when that happens, *workers are alienated from their labor.* That means they work like slaves to make other people rich. The communists think the workers are someday going to get fed up. There will be a wave of revolution sweeping over America and the whole west. The workers will own the factories and the rich folk will have to roll up their sleeves and do some real work."

I saw conversion on a few faces. Sergeant Rodrigues was waving his arms. He waved his arms when he was mad. I thought I better wrap things up. "Understand none of this is true, but you need to know it because that's how the communists over there in Vietnam think." I had no idea how they thought, but it seemed like a safe way to end. I looked at Sergeant Rodrigues. His face needed no interpretation, homicide was written everywhere.

I brought a quick end to the class. "Are there any questions...good...class dismissed."

I made a play for the side door. He caught me halfway down the aisle and hauled me outside. He threw his arms about and let out a Spanish–English stream of invective. I thought he would turn himself inside out. I had disobeyed his order, I was a traitor to my country, I should be in jail. I pretended not to understand a word he was saying, which made him even madder. After I said a second time, "Sergeant, I can't understand you," he waved for me to follow and marched me down the street into the office of the company commander. By the time we arrived, he was calmer, presumably having organized his thoughts on the way. "Captain, Sergeant Howard, he got sick, so he could not teach...on communism. So I see in the file this trainee has a big education, so I say to him, you teach on communism. He say OK, so I think OK. He say today at class the communists are good guys. They know what is best. You got money you are no good. America is no good. I come here from Mexico, I know for sure what is no good. He says people will shoot other people because they can't buy coal. I did not know he would say such things." The sergeant looked at me. "He is no good."

When the sergeant had worn himself out the captain said, "Thank you, Sergeant Rodrigues, I'll handle it from here." He watched the sergeant leave and looked at me for a long moment. "Well, what have you got to say for yourself, Private?"

I stuck to the facts that were in my favor. "Sir, yesterday Sergeant Rodrigues told me I had to teach a class on communism, and that is what I did."

"Private...Gaydos is it? Sounds to me like you incited

violence against the United States government. Some would call that treason."

"Sir, I did not suggest violence. But I might have said there was room for improvement."

He looked at me across another long silence. "Get the hell out of my office."

The Pharmacist

Advanced Individual Training taught the occupational specialties, such as radar, maintenance, intelligence, infantry and all the other jobs that had to be done in the Army. But AIT for people going to Officer Candidacy School was different. It was a warm-up for OCS, and it started with organized harassment. We returned to our barracks to find bunks torn up and bedding scattered across the room. We got up in the middle of the night for forced marches into the countryside. We scrubbed the underside of shower drains with toothbrushes. If socks were not folded just right the punishment was midnight guard duty.

The program continued with classes on command structure: how many men to a platoon, how many platoons to a company, how many companies to a battalion, and so on to the upper reaches of military deity. We delved into the intricacies of S1 Military Staff: the bi-directional flow of information between the commanding officer and subordinate military units. We learned the functioning of S2 Intelligence, S3 Operations and S4 Supply. We sat through endless lectures on the Uniform Code of Military Justice, from which we discovered the military could pretty much do with us what it wanted. As a result of this advanced training we learned to hate the Army more than we thought possible.

We nurtured attitudes of young men who had taken the time and money to attend college, but now found themselves drafted or coerced into the military, soon to be packed off to Vietnam. We took a devil's delight in ridiculing every stick and nail of the program. We were careful to appear in wrinkled uniforms, made an art of marching out of step, snickered at our superiors and used our brains to earn a precise D+ on tests. It was a war of attrition. The more havoc we created, the more we invited surprise inspections and guard duty. But we held strong to the barricades. "What are they gonna do, send us to Vietnam?"

A new lieutenant appeared at morning formation. He walked with his hands in his pockets. The uniform hung on him, like a teenager in his dad's suit. "At ease," he said. The group was already at a sloppy state of attention, so when the "at ease" command came no one moved. This was a planned maneuver and it usually drove the officer wild.

The lieutenant laughed. "Nice, I like it. Shows organization and discipline. Also creativity. A+."

He strolled to the front of the formation, his head down. "I'm your new officer in charge. But I gotta be honest." He raised his head. "I don't know what the fuck I'm doing."

We were shocked. Officers did not use the F-word, much less confess to a weakness of any sort.

He looked at the sky. "The goddamn Army pulls me out of pharmacy school, dresses me in this joke of a costume and tells me to go out there and be a commissioned officer." He threw his arms wide. "I'm fucking lost. You know where I qualified with the M14? A question mark. Shit, they don't even have a question mark category. Some wise guy invented it just for me."

Tittering rippled through the formation. "Pills. Now I know pills. Hell, I could get the whole fucking Viet Cong and the North Vietnamese Army high and end this goddamn war right now."

The formation clapped. Some guy whistled. Another shouted, "How about us too?"

"As long as I'm talking about the war, is this whole situation butt-fucked or what? You go over there, no idea why. Get your ass shot off. Maybe die. No American pussy for a year. And for what?"

A dozen fists came up and a chant started, "Yes…Yes… Yes…" Arms pumped the air. The chant grew louder.

"OK guys, cool it." The lieutenant came close and whispered, "There's big ears around the corner." The formation relaxed into a circle around him. "I got a proposition for you. You don't have to do it if you don't want. Go back and talk about it, but here's the deal. If you guys start to look good in public and get good grades, you can have the run of the place. I'll make sure nobody bothers you. Hell, you can screw your favorite sheep in the barracks if you want to. But you got to make me look good. It's the only way I know not to mess up this assignment like I did the last one."

It seemed a fair exchange. The lieutenant was true to his word and so were we. Harassment stopped overnight. Grades shot up. Starched uniforms became the norm, creased in all the right places. Marching formations tightened and moved with military snap. Soon the college malcontents, the bomb-throwing revolutionaries, were the sharpest unit on the post. Whatever his superiors thought of the lieutenant, to this AIT class he was a genuine leader of men.

Ralph

He was a genius at playing the system, and the smartest guy I knew in the Army. I first came to appreciate Ralph's ability in the small competitions we had with one another, like who could cheat his way farthest up the chow line. Trainees spent forty-five minutes waiting in the rain outside the mess hall and ten minutes eating, so the benefit was substantial. We would shoulder and sneak our way forward one body at a time, maybe saving ten minutes.

Then Ralph upped the game. He took the green tabs off the epaulettes of his fatigue jacket that marked us as trainees. In full view of the sergeants he swaggered to the head of the line and said to the trainee standing there, "Step back, smack head." Hardly breaking stride he walked by the signature desk and threw a wavy line on the sheet. He looked back over his shoulder at me with a grin. Ralph gave this performance over and over. I waited for someone to notice that he did not have a shred of rank on his sleeve, but he pulled it off every time. He was more than a genius. He was without fear or compunction of any kind.

The food in trainee units was awful, balanced by the fact that there was a lot of it. We ate off metal trays with depressed sections for different dollops of food. We shuffled in line so close I could feel the edge of the tray of the guy behind in the small of my back. Sergeants yelled, "Tighten up. Make your buddy smile." The cooks threw food on tray after tray saying, "Move along…move along." We sat elbow-to-elbow, heads bent to the trays as we shoveled food. There was no time for conversation. Sergeants walked along the aisles yelling, "Let's go…let's go…let's go. Hurry up." The room echoed with the noise of forks hitting metal trays and the chewing sounds of a barnyard.

One Sunday morning as we were walking to breakfast Ralph stopped, thought for a moment, and said, "Come…follow me," like he was the messiah. As we walked, Ralph again pulled off his training tabs. "Get rid of yours too. We're going be real soldiers and have us a real breakfast."

Ralph stopped in front of the mess hall belonging to a neighboring battalion of permanent staff, people not in training and with real jobs. There was no line. Ralph pointed his chin at the building, "I am informed the cuisine here is most acceptable." As he started up the steps he added, "Don't sign your real name."

Ralph was already past the sign-in desk and headed for the food line while I stood looking at the clerk behind the desk. The only name I could think to write belonged to a Lebanese great aunt, maybe because it always sounded like music to me. I wrote *Futeen Shalhoub* in clear, rounded penmanship. I thought making it legible would make it believable.

In this mess hall there were real plates. The food line offered sausage, bacon, French toast, hash browns, butter, preserves, grits, coffee and three different juices. The server at the first station asked, "How would you like your eggs?"

It was a question I never expected to be asked in the Army and for a moment could not answer. "Uh…can I have scrambled?"

Little pots of plastic flowers sat on the tables and music played in the background. No one was yelling. So this was the *Other Army*. From that day Private Shalhoub dined there regularly on Sunday morning with his companion Private R. Edward Lee.

Sometimes Ralph got caught, but the boy could turn any situation to his advantage. After one caper gone bad, he got weekend duty at battalion headquarters. But Ralph had a plan; he always had a plan. He asked if he could clean the bathrooms. No soldier in the history of the military had ever asked for toilet duty. Ralph made the little rooms sparkle. He took a toothbrush to corners and crevices. He polished the porcelain fixtures to a white dazzle. He went off-post to buy bars of soap with brand logos etched into their surfaces. He sprayed a subtle but manly scent in the air. As a further surprise Ralph polished the floors of the office to be more mirrors than walking surfaces.

The staff returned on Monday morning to find their world transformed. Among those taking notice was the battalion commander. He said, "Who the hell did all this?" Soon Ralph was helping with paperwork. And then long past his period of punishment he was filling in as the weekend battalion clerk. During the week Ralph was a monkey-dung trainee, and on Sunday he ran battalion headquarters.

Ralph and I went to Vietnam on the same plane. I ended up at LZ Sherry in the middle of the hottest combat area in the Central Highlands.

Ralph became a battalion clerk.

In Love

I met Kathleen on a blind date while on leave in St. Louis. I did not know why she agreed to go out with me. I was a soldier on his way to Vietnam. I had no hair, no money and no prospects. What was this good Catholic girl from south St. Louis thinking? Her parents welcomed me into the living room and invited me to relax on the sofa. A petite Irish beauty walked into the room wearing a pair of low hip huggers in brown plaid. I was in love. But she had forgotten something, so she turned her back and wiggled out of the room. Oh my, now I was in lust.

We went to a drive-in movie with my cousin Mary and her date. Afterward we spent the night talking. Morning dawned, and rather than go home we attended early Sunday mass. We returned to Kathleen's house just as her parents were getting up for mass themselves. We said we had already gone to church, and they pretended to believe us.

I spent the entire week with Kathleen. I cannot remember exactly what we did together or where we went, but I remember we talked and talked. I left for Ft. Sill at the last possible moment, timing the trip to report for duty the next morning.

61

Returning to the fort was like going into the Army for the first time again. I got in at five in the morning, threw on fatigues and reported for duty. The sergeant said to me, "You look like shit. At lunch time go shave. And get a haircut."

Two days later I wrote the first of many letters to Kathleen.

> If this letter is a bit soggy it is because this typewriter just got rained on. But I figure a soggy letter is better than no letter. The spacer goes wild on occasion, and the stationary is upside down and backwards because that is the only way the roller will accept it. Besides all of the above, it's rusty!
>
> The trip back to Ft. Sill was long and lonely after a week with this Kathleen Nash. I am getting slowly used to the grim reality that I am indeed in the Army. Send me a good sexy picture of yourself, or should I say a good picture of your sexy self. I think a lot about you.

Kathleen sent the picture, which I hung in the barracks. Everybody fell in love with her.

Airborne!

Tom was from north St. Louis, a part of the city that could have been in another state to a kid like me from the south side. Despite our geographic differences Tom and I became fast friends. He was everything I was not. He was the Pillsbury Doughboy to my Ichabod Crane. He was careful and detailed to my lofty thinking. He had a plan when I would rather wait for things to happen. He was German to the core, while I inherited the ways of the desert from my Lebanese grandparents. Tom came from a sheltered background and discovered in the Army a doorway to doing things beyond his boyhood imagination.

He began by jumping out of an airplane. Ft. Sill offered the chance to go up in a plane and jump out the door to anyone who went through the training. Tom was giddy with excitement. He tried to convince me to go along with him, but I heard you had to pack your own parachute. If I ever had to jump from a plane I did not want my parachute packed by a dreamhead like myself. This was a minor detail to Tom.

Tom spent the next two weeks in ground exercises: packing his silk, jumping from a low platform to get the feel of hitting and rolling. In the evening he insisted on describing every detail, even acting out the hit and roll on the barracks floor. Tom was doubly prepared. But would he have the guts to jump? Practicing on the ground was one thing, jumping from a plane high enough over central Oklahoma to see Texas was another. One Saturday afternoon I found a note on my bunk. It was un-signed and written in large block letters.

I DID IT

After that Tom walked with a new confidence that was hard to describe but impossible to miss.

Sex was next on Tom's list, and he saw his opportunity in an upcoming international pop festival outside Dallas, an easy drive from Ft. Sill. We hit the road on Saturday morning in my VW Beetle. The whole trip Tom could not stop talking about tie dyed halter tops, skinny dipping and carnival sex.

The festival was a 60s classic: 200,000 long-haired hip-pies camped in a large field beneath a hanging cloud of mari-juana smoke. Tom caught news of rampant skinny dipping at a nearby reservoir, and took off like a happy puppy. "See ya later," was all I heard from the guy who normally had to have a plan for going to the bathroom.

I was more interested in finding a good spot up by the stage for the music. I pushed my way through psychedelic bell-bottom pants, peace tattoos and headbands, all the while feeling conspicuous in my white jeans and Ban-Lon shirt. Once I had secured my piece of ground, I did my best to blend in with the natives. I stripped off my shirt, mussed up the pitiful patch of hair on the top of my head and put on sandals. Then I saw a group of guys looking a lot like me sitting in a circle and passing around a joint. They turned out to be warrant officer candidates from Fort Gordon. I thought, *we're all from the same box of cookies*.

The music took me to another world. Here in front of me, almost close enough to touch, were the icons, the heroes, the gods of music that until now existed only in the vinyl records in their cardboard covers on my shelf at home. First came Herbie Mann, and in succession Sam and Dave, Bonnie & Friends, B.B. King, Delaney, and the day's headliner, Led Zeppelin, who brought the crowd to its feet with "Whole Lotta Love."

I met up with Tom later that night at the car. He was bubbling with excitement. "Soon as I left you I saw a girl, up close, dancing topless. Then over in a corner I saw some guy balling his girl, and there were people standing around cheering. The girls are so easy I can't believe it. So I went up to these two girls and was getting ready to see if I could buy them a Coke, when these two other guys came up and asked if they were taken for the evening. And they just up and went off with them."

Tom was aflame with the possibilities. "Tomorrow night I'm definitely going to get a girl. If you don't mind I'm going to bring her back to the car. I'll have to get a short one to fit into the back seat. I'll say, 'Are you with anybody? Good... you are now.' Then later when it gets dark I'll say, 'We're just going to throw some blankets on the ground for tonight, you can stay with me...if that's all right with you.' When it starts to get chilly that's when we go into the car." He paused, a little breathless, and said, " What do you think?"

"It all seems a little too direct," I said. I was no expert, but I knew the caveman approach probably wouldn't work. "Why don't you ask if you can hang out with her, or just say something about the music and keep talking. Something like that."

We rehearsed a number of opening lines. Tom said the whole thing was no different than jumping out of an airplane. You just had to practice and do it by the numbers. When he got comfortable with his script he said, "So now what do you think?"

"Can't miss."

That evening Tom returned earlier than expected. He said, "I spotted the perfect girl. Cute and not too tall. So I went up to her and said, 'Pardon me, but would you like some company?' just like we practiced." He took a little swallow. "She looked up at me and said, 'I don't mind but you'll have to ask my father over there.'"

Road Guard

In Advanced Individual Training we played at being officers. We had to pretend it meant somthing, like a toy steering wheel on a car seat. Lieutenants led a platoon of twelve trainees. Captains were over a company of four platoons. Colonels commanded battalions and brigades. The officers wore felt patches of different colors on their jacket epaulettes to show their rank. Enlisted men saluted these make-believe officers, who led them from classroom to classroom as if on combat missions.

I was a full bird colonel and battalion commander, signified by a red felt patch on each shoulder. I did not do anything to earn this rank. Someone needed to play the colonel and I happened to be standing around with nothing better to do. I was the ideal pretend colonel. I stood tall and slim in a flawless uniform. I had good grades. I made correct salutes, careful to hold the hand tilted down so as not to show the palm like the prissy British saluted.

But I had a problem. I no longer wanted to attend OCS. If officer training was going to be anything like AIT, it wasn't worth an extra ten months in the military. I first had to tell my lieutenant. Standing in his signature slouch he said, "OK, I understand. I wish I wasn't an officer, but you know that already."

The company captain, the real one, tried for an hour to make me change my mind. Then he hauled me off to the battalion executive officer, a major who got nasty with me. "Soldier, you're making a very stupid decision," he said. I thought of telling him he was talking to a superior officer. *No, just get out of his office.*

The next morning at formation I got busted from colonel down to road guard. Instead of spiffy red tabs, I had to wear an orange vest. The major wanted to make an example of what happens to quitters. The lieutenant would have none of it. He came to the formation wearing his dress green uniform instead of the standard fatigues. This uniform fit him. He looked taller than usual. He carried the orange vest in two upturned hands, as if it were a sacred garment. He called the formation to attention and instructed me to step forward. He placed the vest over my head and helped to secure the ties around my waist, like an altar boy helping the priest get into his vestments. The lieutenant stepped back, came to attention and did something an officer should never do. He initiated the salute to an enlisted man. He held his salute until I lowered mine, another scandalous reversal of military etiquette. "Specialist Gaydos," he said, "congratulations. We are proud of you." A cheer went up from the formation still at attention.

When the company marched from one location to another I ran ahead to intersections and stopped traffic. I made a show of it. Stepping into the traffic I raised two arms to stop vehicles from both directions. I enjoyed seeing cars driven by sergeants, captains and majors obey my command. I always turned my head to watch the men crossing behind me. I held the cars for a moment longer than I had to, a small abuse of authority, before impatiently waving them along. "Come on…come on…come on." Then I was off at a dead run for the next intersection, elbows pumping and orange vest flapping. After company clerk, road guard was the best job I ever had in the military.

Moving Down in the World

What would become of me now that I would never be an officer? I learned that I was not eligible for clean, safe jobs like intelligence or public relations, because signing up for officer training had committed me irrevocably to a combat specialty. I had solid reason to believe the Army would send me to infantry training at Ft. Benning in Georgia. Early in basic training I had taken a battery of tests on intelligence, personality and interests. My profile came back saying I was most suited for "Infantry Officer." At the time I was relieved that I had wisely enlisted for combat engineering. Now I imagined a clerk pulling my file and thinking, *This weenie chickened out of officer school; at least we can put him where he belongs with the weed wigglers.* I seemed to be sliding down a greased ramp with the deadly jungles and rice paddies of Vietnam at its bottom. Why did I not join the Air Force when I had the chance? And why in heaven's name had I left the seminary for a life with women? Sure, I had met Kathleen, but now I was headed for a tour of combat celibacy, a lot more dangerous than being a monk and with largely the same outcome.

In the midst of this anguish, I came across something at Ft. Sill that was a minor salvation: Artillery Combat Leadership school. ACL taught the same technical skills as officer school, but involved none of the harassment, and it required no additional time in the service. At the end, graduates were promoted to E5, or sergeant grade. I would be out of the military in two years with a little bit of rank on my sleeve. There was only one downside. Graduates went straight to Vietnam artillery units, where they were greeted as "shake 'n' bakes." I figured I was going to Vietnam anyway. It would take six months to get through the training, and again I hoped maybe the war would end. Maybe I would get with a unit eight miles from the fighting, or maybe I could snag a clerk job. My life hung on a thin string of *maybes*.

Fire Watch

The barracks buildings of my new school were thrown up early in WWII to house the flood of men coming into the Army. These were to be temporary structures, two stories of light framing and slat siding nailed up in a hurry. Thirty years later they still stood, arthritic and feeble. At night the wind screamed through the window frame at the foot of my bunk. During the bitterest weeks I slept fully clothed in a fatigue jacket, wool cap and gloves. In the morning I often found a light dusting of snow over me.

The furnace was as old as the building, and wheezed a trickle of heat into the barracks, or as often decided not to work at all. Our sergeant addressed the furnace problem by ignoring it. After a week without heat a trainee from California with a law degree told the sergeant that he was writing to his congress-man. He wanted to make sure he spelled the sergeant's name correctly. A technician showed up the next day, but two days later the furnace was out again.

One evening as we faced another frigid night without heat, a trainee who knew a little about furnaces said, "I'll take a

72

look if you guys want. Hell, I can't make it any colder."

The utility room was padlocked, but a shoulder against the door pulled the lock hinge neatly from the frame. Our man poked around the furnace with a flashlight, his breath blowing silver puffs into the air. He asked if anyone had a piece of wire or a paperclip. Within minutes the heat began to flow, at least enough to keep the barracks above freezing. "Just a little trick I learned," he said. "But we're gonna want to keep a close watch out for the thing catching on fire."

The next morning when the sergeant walked into the barracks he looked at the broken lock. "What the hell happened here?"

Our Stanford law graduate spoke for the group. "It's pretty clear, Sergeant. We broke into the utility room so we could fix the furnace."

"That's an unauthorized area. Can't you read the fuckin' sign on the door? It's also destroying government property. I want to know who's responsible."

Stanford said, "All of us. We have a right to heat in the barracks."

"You don't have a right to shit. You're in the Army, and I own your asses."

"You can have all of my ass that you want, Sergeant, if that's your inclination. But another lock goes on that door, we're going to break in again."

"You do and I'll have the bunch of you in front of the company commander, and he is not a nice man."

Stanford softened his tone. "Sergeant, look. It's only a furnace, and we figured out how to keep it going. And I don't want to keep writing letters to Washington because you're not doing your job. As far as I'm concerned, that door looks perfectly secured."

The room stayed unlocked. With it remained the very real possibility that the furnace might explode.

The building had no fire alarms or sprinkler system. A fire would consume the structure in minutes, and us along with it. The Army's solution was to place buckets of sand along the wall between every other bed. At night there was a fire guard rotation. One trainee sat up for an hour and then woke up the guy in the next bunk. Fire duty came around every three or four days. It was a wonderful night when I knew I would not be shaken awake at 2:00 a.m. to stare into the dark for an hour.

One night I did a shameful thing. I woke up the guy in the next bunk and went right back to sleep. At the time it seemed like a victimless crime. In the morning it was clear to the person shaken awake at 5:00 a.m., who was not supposed to have a watch, that someone had skipped his turn. Outraged and bellowing he went hunting for the culprit. It was an easy calculation to find me, but the guy never managed to figure it out. I got away with a misdeed, but felt awful about it. The next time my turn came around I did two hours. The guy who was not called, and should have been, did not come looking.

Captain Bill

Artillery Combat Leadership school taught us a lot about artillery, a little about combat and nothing about leadership. It began with more instruction on advanced marching, such as executing a *column left*. We moved to more work on executing the command voice, so vital to becoming a leader of men. I could never get out a "Ten-HUT" without sounding like a college professor. Twenty hours of instruction went to maintenance forms. We spent four hours on form DA 2408-1, the monthly equipment log. I wrote to Kathleen that I was "so bored I got an upset stomach."

In the early weeks of the program the instructors were a parade of clowns. One instructor, a career sergeant, flashed slides on the screen and said, "Any questions about what's on the screen there? It's self explanatory." We soon wondered among ourselves if he could read. To keep our attention he randomly slipped nudie pictures into the slide deck.

A fat sergeant recently returned from Vietnam taught the class on battery organization. The class was supposed to cover equipment levels, staffing and the role of attached units such as medical corps and radar. Instead he spent the class complaining about the people in the mess bunker eating up extra chow.

Another told Vietnam war stories, summing up his tour in Vietnam as a constant round of "getting drunk and getting laid."

The most colorful instructor was a black sergeant from Mississippi. He was a preacher before the Army and loved to tell of emptying his M16 rifle at the Viet Cong. As he warmed to the topic he began to sing his words and throw his arms wide to the heavens, carried away with the memory of the rifle pulsing in his hands and the blood of the heathen spattering the jungle foliage.

One of the students shouted, "Alleluia, alleluia."

"Amen, brother," he said in return. He planned on going back to his small church in Mississippi after the Army.

Within a short time the training turned serious. A major spent an entire day with us on perimeter defense of an artillery firebase, something everybody would face. He talked about rocket and mortar fire. He described ground attacks initiated by Vietnamese guerillas that he called sappers. They would slip through the barbed wire with satchel charges strapped across their chests. He showed us pictures of the coils of concertina wire that surrounded a firebase. There were waves of them and they looked impregnable. Then the major showed a film of a sapper crawling and wriggling his way through the wire in less than a minute. He said, "The sapper blows the wire and opens the way for VC regulars to come through. If Charlie is organized and prepared, he can put the hurt on you. Vietnam is months of tedium and boredom punctuated by moments of terror." I had heard that said before about war, and guessed Vietnam would be no different.

CAPTAIN BILL

William Beach was the gunnery instructor, and we called him Captain Bill. He was just back from Vietnam, where sun and hard living had aged his face beyond its years. It was a face that nothing surprised anymore. He taught at the blackboard without a note and never needed a pencil to figure a number. He had the body of a shortstop and moved around the classroom scooping up questions, firing off answers and lobbing questions of his own. "Tube memory. Why does a howitzer fire a little farther than it should immediately after a long shot?" Silence. "Well I'll tell you. We have no idea. It just does and you better figure it in."

Computing data for firing an artillery piece went by the mouthful "fire direction control," FDC for short, and proved more complicated than anyone imagined. There was map reading and learning instruments that measured distance, direction and altitude. We had to master calculations involving type of projectile, distance to the target, target altitude, the number of rounds the tube had already fired, projectile spin, humidity, air temperature, wind direction and speed, height of detonation, the rotation of the earth, and of course the ever popular tube memory. Each adjustment had a special chart or graph. We drilled endlessly on the protocol for communicating with the guns. It was a precise language with steps from the beginning of a fire mission to its end. We had hours of evening homework. The work grew more difficult every week, and every week one or two trainees dropped out.

Captain Bill liked teaching, but he lived for action. His first priority was to show us what it felt like on the receiving end of a howitzer. He took us to the middle of the firing range, a desolate stretch of Oklahoma scrub country. We packed into a dirt bunker that looked like just another hill and donned steel pot helmets and flak jackets.

"Don't forget your earplugs," the captain said. "You're going to need them."

A few of us had a view out of narrow slits in the wall, but most crowded into the middle of the bunker. The roof was so low I could barely stand upright and had to crouch to see out one of the slits.

"OK, girls, listen up," the captain said. "In Vietnam most of you are going to be in Fire Direction Control, on the shooting end. Some of you are going to be forward observers out with the infantry and calling in fire. But all of you need to know how close you can get with artillery before it gets interesting. Thirty meters may seem like a long way off, but let's see." He pulled a radio handset from its box on the wall. "This goes to a 155mm howitzer, as you know not the biggest tube in the Army, but not the smallest either. It's locked in on a fixed target thirty meters to our front. Are you ready?"

Nobody said anything. The captain grinned as he said, "Fire" into the handset. He kept the handset to his ear. "Shot," he said. "Payload's in the air." He kept looking at us with that grin. He said, "Splash. Hold onto your jocks." An explosion seemed to lift the bunker into the air. A white flash showed through the slit and a fist of sound hit my chest. Shrapnel splattered the bunker like death knocking at the door. The air tasted metallic and felt prickly on the skin. The smell of gunpowder filled the little bunker.

"Holy shit," someone said.

Another explosion shook the earth. And another. By then we were huddled in the middle of the floor, some guys sitting with their heads between their legs and holding onto their helmets.

"Check fire," I heard the captain say. "Anybody want some more?" When nobody volunteered, he said into the handset, "End mission."

The captain led us outside. "Fall in at ease, I want to say something." He pulled himself tall and said, "Now you know why the artillery is the king of battle—because it kills the most people. It's not a toy. You men are going to be in charge of where this stuff lands. A little mistake or a lazy shortcut can move a round a hundred meters left or right, and now you know what that can do. Your little slip-ups can kill the wrong people. Tomorrow you're coming back here and you're gonna practice killing the right people."

Early the next morning in the dim chill he took us to a hill overlooking the same firing range. One soldier carried a radio on his back. The rest of us had the standard issue equipment for a forward observer: calibrated binoculars, grease pencil, compass and map. The sun had just come up when Captain Bill said, "You are attached to an infantry platoon as an artillery forward observer. Your battery is indicated on your map, and so is the radio frequency of fire direction control. For this mission your call sign is "Huge Member" and FDC's is "Sugar Momma". That old truck out there is Charlie and he is kicking your ass. Make Charlie go away."

We called up the mission and followed protocol. We gave the map coordinates and ordered a marking smoke round. A mushroom of gray smoke erupted 200 yards behind Charlie. The next round would be high explosive, HE. We sent in the command to change rounds and adjust, "Hotel echo, add two zero zero, repeat." The round cracked white and blossomed in a black cloud, but now 100 yards in front of the target.

Good but not good enough. "Drop one zero zero, repeat."

We waited. Nothing.

The radio operator called in, "Sugar Momma, you got a problem?"

There was a long pause, and then the reply, "Huge Member, hold." Another minute went by. "Huge Member, shot." We waited for the "splash" message giving us ten seconds to take cover. Instead the air in front of us exploded and something went loud and growling past my right ear. I dropped to the ground and felt the burn of gunpowder in my nose and eyes. The inside of my mouth turned bitter.

"What the fuck was that?" someone yelled.

The captain's voice came, "That, gentlemen, was bad data."

We ended the mission and the captain got us to our feet. "We'll worry about that later, but my guess is Sugar Momma added one zero zero instead of dropping it. Then again, maybe that's what you told her to do." We looked at each other with blank stares.

The captain had no time for more talk. "It's not over, boys. Charlie just forced you off your position and like sorry shits you lost your binoculars." He collected the binoculars and walked to a spot fifty yards along the side of the hill. "Charlie is kicking your ass and laughing. Call in another mission. And try not to blow yourself up."

We took cover this time and were careful with adjustments. The captain moved us to a third location, now taking away our maps and grease pencils. "You college boys should have no trouble figuring things out." Captain Bill was starting to enjoy himself. At the next stop another fifty yards away he took the compasses, leaving us with only the two eyes God gave us for calling in fire. We surprised ourselves with how close we could land a round to the target just by estimating distances and compass directions.

"You ain't done yet. Everybody turn around and face the hill. Charlie's now got you pinned down and separated from your platoon. Your guys are off to your rear a hundred meters and Charlie is seventy-five meters to their east. Do your stuff." With our backs to the impact area and with no equipment but a radio, we called in fire on a target we could not see, adjusting by the sound of the impacts behind us. We heard the captain say, "You're inside the fifty meter kill zone. Good job. Move out."

The captain thought the exercise was over, but not by our reckoning. "Sir, we don't want to leave without a direct hit."

He sat down on the ground and said, "The mission is still open. Let me know when you're done playing."

We turned to face the target and called in another adjustment. Close, but missed again. From his seat, the captain said, "How much government money do you monkeys plan to waste? More important, I have a date tonight."

On the third adjustment we got lucky. The round caught the truck at the right front tire, sending it flipping into the air.

"May we move out now, ladies?" Captain Bill asked.

As we were coming off the hill, a band of deer wandered into the far edge of the firing range. The captain stopped us, "Let's see how good you guys really are."

"Is that legal, sir? Hunting with a howitzer?"

"I have no idea."

We called up a fresh fire mission on the deer, little boys playing with a deadly toy. The first round, a high explosive air burst, brought down three and left them twitching on the ground. Some guys thought this was cruel, and said so.

81

"Yeah, it's not nice," said the captain. "Neither is shooting up gooks. But gooks are more fun because they shoot back."

Two days later Captain Bill took us back to the mountain for a night shoot. We looked into solid black, figuring the firing range was down there somewhere. An illumination round popped high in the air. It hung below a tiny parachute and lit the valley. I thought of night baseball games at Busch Stadium in St. Louis, the Cardinals against the Cubbies. Our targets were the same derelict jeeps and trucks. But now they looked almost alive as the descending illumination shifted shadows around them. Calling in the mission was more difficult than we anticipated. We had to juggle flashlights as we manipulated maps and compasses. The target area faded to black again when the illumination round fizzled into the ground. We waited for the next to pop, and then hurried our work as the targets seemed to move on their own before melting into the night. Captain Bill liked to see us fumble with the maps and curse our equipment. "This is the easy part, men. It's not raining, and the gooks are not lobbing mortars or tossing AK47 at you."

In three days we were back on the mountain again. Captain Bill was in a good mood, which was never a good sign. "Your FDC has gone dark. That means a rocket or a mortar or maybe even a satchel charge knocked it out. So now you figure up your own data, and you talk directly to the guns. All that stuff your Sugar Momma has been doing for you with slide rulers and tables, now you have to do it in your head. Gentlemen, welcome to black magic."

"Sir, that's impossible. How do we know what to tell the guns?"

"You've computed firing data before."

"But we don't have a range deflection protractor or the

82

graphical firing…"

"Yeah I know," that big grin back again. "But you have a map. That's all you need. Figure it out."

We knew where the howitzers were and remembered from class that the 155 had a maximum range of about nine miles. After some discussion we agreed on the elevation and direction we wanted the howitzer to shoot. There was one big problem. Howitzer crews did not aim the gun by a compass direction. They went by deflection off an aiming stick planted in the ground out in front of the gun. The radio operator at the gun came back at us with, "We need a deflection. A direction don't do us a damn bit of good."

"We got to find out the azimuth of that damn aiming stick or those gun bunnies are going to be useless." It was our radio operator talking. He said into his handset, "Go get your crew chief." After a short pause he said, "Sergeant, we got an aiming stick problem. Do you know what azimuth the battery is laid on? OK then, do you have a compass? I don't know why you would have a compass. Forget the compass. Stand behind the gun and look at the aiming stick. Can you see anything behind the stick, like a high hill or a bend in a creek, anything like that? Yeah I know, it's dark here too, but try. A water tower a little to the left…great. Hold on, sergeant, we'll have your deflection for you in a minute." We got the water tower on the map, figured the direction the battery was oriented and from there got a deflection close enough to get a smoke round in the air.

When the radio operator gave the "fire" command we headed for cover. There was no telling where the round would land, on top of us or in the next county. We would have been thrilled just to see the round, and were shocked when it hit only 200 yards off target. From there it was easy to adjust with a couple more smoke rounds and call in high explosive.

On the march back to the barracks the captain was quiet. No "good job" or "nice work." We knew we had nailed it. He knew we knew, and that was enough. We had learned that a howitzer was not an inert collection of parts, but a living thing that could be coaxed into doing whatever the mind of the artilleryman could imagine. There was not much more he could teach us.

Captain Bill was hanging a chart in class one day when he said, "After the Army I can always be a paperhanger."

Someone shot back, "Or a contract killer." He did not disagree.

To the Rear March

Our sergeant liked to call the Catholics in the class "mackerel snappers," for our practice of eating fish on Friday. He said it with a pig-eyed malice. I was a double offender, because I also played on the battalion basketball team. The colonel had high hopes for the team and made practices a priority. It drove the sergeant mad when I left for practice in the middle of training. When the time came to get volunteers for a special drill team, he was on me with a mean glint in his eye.

"This training company," he announced at formation, "has been chosen to perform a silent drill at an upcoming graduation ceremony. The post commander and his staff will be there, and I need twelve volunteers." Only a few arms went into the air. I learned on the first day of basic training never to raise my hand. No good could come of it. The sergeant walked along the rows of soldiers and stopped in front of me. "Put up your hand, Specialist Gaydos." I gave him the look I learned in basic. But he kept at it. "Put up your hand." And I kept at it with the look. He got up close to my face, but said loud enough for everybody to hear, "You are volunteering whether you want to or not. The whole company is going to stand here in the cold until you do."

Groans went up along the ranks. I said, "OK, Sergeant."

Silent drill involved performing complicated marching maneuvers without verbal commands. It was a beautiful thing to watch, soldiers weaving in and out like they were reading one another's minds, something like a marching band performing at halftime. Silent drill was a fragile edifice. One mistake by one person would bring the house down in ruin.

We practiced *column left march* for ten paces, *to the rear march* for fifteen, *halt* for a five count, *about face present arms* for another five count, *forward march* for eight paces. The whole of these silent commands added up to a five-minute routine. We got to a decent level of execution and felt good about ourselves.

The day dawned bitterly cold and snowing. The stands at the parade ground were filled with graduating classes from all over the post. After the post commander finished his remarks, our drill team took to the field. Through the snow the people in the stands appeared as a gray blur. My hands were numb and I had to look at them to know they were holding a rifle.

The sergeant shouted a single command to begin the drill. We were off. I stayed with the proper sequence of movements until I saw through the snow a soldier stepping directly across my line of march. Thinking I had perhaps miscounted the paces, I turned and followed him. Then he was gone, off on some new tangent, leaving me lost in a white wilderness. Someone started to laugh. We bumped into each other, banged rifle barrels and wandered around like souls looking for a light switch in a dark room.

A voice sounded through the curtain of snow, "That's enough, boys."

Later in the barracks the sergeant vented his anger. "I've never been this embarrassed in my career."

Someone said, "Sergeant, if we couldn't see the general, maybe he couldn't see us."

"Oh, he saw you alright. Told the company commander he had seen enough. That's why it ended. What a cluster fuck! And I mean that literally."

I raised my hand. "Sergeant, I have to go. I got basketball practice."

Guests of the Viet Cong

The exercise was "Escape and Evasion." It was late January. A thin crust of frost covered the mud and crunched beneath our boots as they sank into the ooze. We were caught behind enemy lines trying to make our way back to friendly forces. The Viet Cong, played by infantrymen just back from Vietnam, were after us. Our mission was to evade capture and make it back to home base. If captured we would end up in a Viet Cong prison camp, where we would see how Charlie treated Yankee dogs.

My band of four guys decided on a flanking maneuver to bring us into home base from the rear. Yes, we would surprise them. We kept low, moving from bush to bush and waiting for any sign of the enemy. On our third scramble to the next hiding place, I came upon shoelaces and looked up into a rifle barrel.

"Consider yourself caught, asshole," said a voice from behind the barrel. "Get on your feet."

When I stood up, so did three guys from surrounding bushes, believing he was talking to them. Our captor looked surprised, "What a bunch of pussies." He pointed with the rifle barrel, "Move off. All of you."

The POW camp was a clearing in the woods and already crowded. Prisoners were laying face down in the mud, their chins just high enough to breathe. Others were blindfolded and squatting back to back. The sound of groaning hung over the camp. Our captors wore standard issue fatigues, not VC pajamas. They all had M16s. Some carried them at their sides in one hand 'Nam fashion. Others held them at the ready, finger inside the trigger guard.

They were fresh from Vietnam, some still with the faraway look that comes from combat. In Vietnam they had lived in muddy uniforms and went days, sometimes weeks, without a shave, a shower or a hot meal. Some had seen buddies die. They now wondered why they were still alive themselves, or why they deserved to be. The only reason they were still in the Army was the time left on two-year commitments. They treated the niceties of stateside duty with contempt, saluting with a raised middle finger or neglecting to salute altogether. What to do with them? They would not be in the Army long enough to have real jobs. There was only menial work and idleness. A few returned to Vietnam to serve out their time. The rest were a burden to an Army that would not let them go, yet had no use for them.

My captor led me off to the side. When he found a muddy spot he sat me down. He said, "You want to get through this, tell him what he wants." Then he squatted down level with my face. "Let me tell you something, college boy. You notice there's no fuckin' officers out here? We got one rule. No visible marks. That leaves a lot of room for fun, if you know what I mean."

I watched them lead prisoners off one at a time into the

woods. There was muffled shouting and low thuds, then silence. Soon another prisoner would get up and be led into the trees. No one returned. The wet of the ground began to work its way into my lower bowel. It felt like a cold finger.

I saw them lead Tom away. The entire front of his uniform was brown with mud, and he was trembling. Tom was not good at this sort of thing. He was just a little boy trying to grow up in the Army, and he believed everything people told him. His courageous leap from an airplane had not prepared him for this. The guy would say something out of a training manual and get a punch in the stomach for his patriotism.

My turn in the woods soon came. The interrogator carried a baseball bat. He was maybe nineteen years old. He backed me up against a tree and circled. He was at my left ear when he screamed, "Gimme your name." With that he swung the bat and hit the tree just behind the small of my back.

I spilled my guts. "Specialist Gaydos."

"What is your unit, imperialist dog?" Another whack on the tree.

So this was the game. I almost laughed. "I'm a trainee. ACL Battalion, Alpha Battery."

"What are your radio codes?" Whack. *That poor tree*, I thought.

"Tango Charlie. No, wait a minute. Maybe it's Charlie Tango. Hold on. I seem to remember there was a Bravo in there somewhere and some numbers. Let me think. OK. Let's go with Bravo Tango Six Niner. You see we picked 69 because the Army has a way of…"

The bat went limp in his arm and he turned to his sergeant. "I am really sick of this shit. Can't I shoot just one of these fuckers?"

The sergeant said, "Maybe tomorrow, soldier."

An open truck on a nearby road collected the prisoners after their interrogations. They sat on benches in the truck bed, like so many pillars of mud. Tom was jabbering away when I climbed up. "...on the tree. Then he said he was going to stick it up my ass, but the sergeant said he couldn't say that. Then he said something about sucking his dick, and the sergeant said not that either. Then he got really pissed and let me go. I didn't have to say a word. You think the VC do that, you know, about the ass and the dick and everything?"

At the barracks several of us walked straight off the truck and into the shower fully dressed. The water ran in a brown river. I was cold to the core and shaking. I stood under the hot water for half an hour before I stopped trembling. The barracks was a tangled heap of C-ration cans, soggy uniforms and exhausted soldiers. The odor of unwashed bodies mingled with the smell of *Beans W/ Meat Balls and Tomato Sauce*.

The sergeant came in and said, "Welcome back, men. I want this place squared away by 1900 hours. I need not remind you of your final exam tomorrow morning."

The Best Dressed Soldier

The battalion colonel presented an award at our graduation ceremony to the trainee who wore the best uniform. I wrote to Kathleen in longhand, as I would for the next year:

The colonel does not like short pants, so our captain called a big inspection Saturday morning before graduation. No socks could be showing and the back of the trouser had to come within an inch of the bottom of the shoe heel.

My greens (dress uniform) fit me beautifully and I had just gotten them cleaned and pressed. I was looking sharp for the inspection. But unfortunately my trousers came nowhere near the floor.

When the captain came to me he said that would never do. He told me to hike my pants down a little, which I did. A little more, and more still. By this time I could no longer see my shoes.

" Can you hike them down a little more?" he said.

" Not without embarrassment, sir "

He was finally satisfied when my crotch fell somewhere around my knees. "Yes, sir. I will be sure to wear them exactly like this for graduation."

The big graduation morning finally dawned with everyone wearing his trousers like he damn well pleased. We all wanted to have a look at the colonel's trousers. They were shorter than anyone's! Not only could you see his socks, you could see his right shin. And the rest of his uniform looked as though he had fought the whole Korean campaign in it.

The winner of the colonel's best-

*dressed award had a pair of trou-
sers certainly long enough, but so
wide and baggy you could throw a
cocktail party in them. He looked
like the "after" of a diet commercial still wearing his "before"
trousers.*

Remember Tom? He's the one.

When the colonel ordered Specialist 5 Thomas Kitta to step forward, I clapped so hard my hands hurt.

Tom and I later shipped out for Vietnam together, but once in country went our separate ways. He sent me a letter after a few weeks saying he was in Cambodia, and then another letter four months later. I wrote to Kathleen:

*I got another letter from Tom.
He's up by Kontum now getting
mortared. He sounded depressed
to me, which is not too surprising. Everybody gets depressed
over here, especially people in
the field.*

Kontum was 250 miles north of LZ Sherry and forty miles from the border with Cambodia. It was the provincial capital and a hot spot. I worried about Tom until I heard he was back in St. Louis in one piece.

The Real Army

I was the honor graduate of my class, which won me an assignment back to the ACL battalion for on-the-job training. OJT was two months of preparation for Vietnam, the last stop before deployment. My job was to supervise a radar platoon of four men. I had to make sure they got to class in the morning, and returned on time to the barracks. That was the whole job.

I soon found I did not even have to march along with my trainees. Like my pharmacist lieutenant, I made a deal with the radar trainees. I said, "You make me look good and I'll leave you alone. That means getting to class on time and marching like you mean it." And just like my class of disgruntled college kids, they took the deal. I watched them leave the barracks in the morning, then hopped into my car, drove to the classroom building, and from the warmth of the front seat watched them arrive. The end of the day was the same. *Never walk when you can ride.*

What did I do with all my free time? I went to the NCO club, secured a table in the corner, bought a pot of coffee and read books. From my table I watched the goings-on at the club.

By the time I arrived there was already a gang of sergeants solidly bivouacked at the bar. Alcohol was so cheap it would have been easier to give it away. None of us stirred all day, except to bend elbows and trot to the bathroom. I came to admire the men at the bar. Anyone who could fritter away the day with his pals, maintain a mild drunk and all the while get paid for it, must have something going for him. The guys at the bar may have been practicing alcoholics, but that did not mean they were stupid. They had to be smart to look like they had real jobs and still do nothing all day. I wished with all my heart to be one of these Knights of the Long Table.

How to Shoot the M16

Four weeks before deploying for Vietnam I got my hands on the M16 rifle, a light piece of plastic that hardly seemed like a weapon at all compared to the bulk of the M14. It was four pounds lighter and seven inches shorter. It had a smaller bullet, making it less effective at longer ranges, but the combined weight of the rifle and ammo allowed the soldier to carry twice the ammunition, a good tradeoff in the close quarters of jungle fighting. The M16 had been standard issue in Vietnam for three years. There were reports about it jamming, and stories that the soldiers hated it. But I fell in love with it. I wrote to Kathleen:

For the past two days I have been out qualifying with the M16 - that innocent looking 6-pound toy I'll be playing with over in sunny Southeast Asia. You can break the whole weapon down with your fingers and a moron could clean and assemble one. It

97

*has the kick of a BB gun with
an effective range of about five
football fields.*

Training on the M16 was my first experience of firing
an automatic rifle. I had trained on a machine gun, the big .50
caliber, but never a fully automatic rifle. In basic training when
shooting the M14, we received one bullet at a time. A range
sergeant walked along the line and watched as we sighted in on
our target and slowly squeezed the trigger. Shooting on fully
automatic was an entirely different experience. A magazine of
twenty rounds emptied in two seconds. The spinning of the bullets as they traveled through the barrel pulled the weapon up
and to the right. We were told to aim at the lower left of the
target and let the pull of the rifle carry the fire up and across the
target. Once we had mastered the technique, the firing sergeant
said to us, "Don't use automatic, unless you're in a really tight
situation. Two seconds is not a lot of fire time and most of your
bullets are not going to hit your target." He said to set the rifle
on semi-automatic and pop out a couple rounds at a time, or
better yet, one at a time. "Look at what you want to hit. Don't
just spray bullets all over the place."

That was clear enough, but then he surprised us. "In Vietnam you're not going to have time to aim, not like at a shooting
range. You'll go more on instinct." In a few words he overturned all the meticulous training we had done on the M14. It
sounded like military heresy. "You can hit any target you want
without aiming. Believe me." Nobody did.

Smiling, he pulled out a Daisy BB gun and then retrieved
a handful of paper plates from his satchel. "OK, first guy up.
All I want you to do is look and react." He took one of the pa-

per plates and tossed it into the air. The soldier watched it settle to the ground. "OK, you got the looking part great. This time shoot at it. But don't aim."

The soldier fired the BB gun from about chest high and nicked the edge of the plate. He said, "Give me another one, sarge. I'll nail it."

We all nailed it. The instructor moved to tin can lids. When we were taking those out of the air with almost no effort, he tossed quarters. Then nickels. Half of us could hit a dime. We were feeling pretty good. "Pay attention," the instructor said. He moved his arm into the air as if he were throwing something but nothing went up. "What did I just throw?"

"Nothing," we all said together.

"Wrong. Watch again."

A voice came from the back of the formation. "Sarge, I think it was a BB."

"Correct. Now everybody watch again." His arm moved. "How many of you saw it this time?" Three hands went up. "Keep watching." Now half a dozen hands went up. The instructor kept tossing a single BB in the air until we could all see it. "Now get in formation and fall in at ease."

We lined up. "Men," he said, "I want you to listen carefully to what I am going to tell you. Here is the point of this entire exercise. Are you ready?" He paused. "If you can see it, you can hit it." He looked at us for a long minute. "I want to hear you shout it, 'If I can see it, I can hit it.' Now sound off."

At our first weak attempt he became a drill sergeant. "I CAN'T HEEEEEEAR YOU." When we were loud enough to suit him, he shortened the sound-off to a chant. "See it, hit it. See it, hit it." We began to sway with the rhythm, and soon went into a war dance, stomping left and right to the cadence of

"See...hit...see...hit."

The instructor cut in, "Check fire. Now let's see how many of you can do it."

We jostled one another to be first. "You each get ten tries," the instructor said. "It's all about seeing. Believe this."

I did not think it could be done, until the first soldier connected near the end of his turn. A cheer went up. I hit only one on my turn. With my lousy eyes the BBs looked like furry brown things. Except for the one I hit. It was a copper dot frozen in mid air. A click and it was gone. The best in our group hit four out of ten.

The instructor told us the post record was five. "One of these days some boy out of Tennessee is going to come along and get all ten."

Ready for Combat

The last preparation for Vietnam was getting inoculations against the exotic diseases in that part of the world, many of which were unknown to western medicine. There were so many shots and tests I surrendered my body to the medics without paying much attention. However I took the time to read my dog tags after a blood test, and saw that the blood type was wrong. This was a detail that seemed important to get right. I said to one of the medical techs, "Corporal, my blood type is wrong on these tags."

"Let me see them." He studied them and said, "You're O-negative."

"I'm O-positive."

"The tags say you're O-negative."

"That's what I'm trying to tell you, the tags are wrong."

"They can't be, we tested your blood."

"I know my blood type. It's O-positive."

He puffed and went off for the paperwork. "See, it says here you're O-negative. It's what the test said, so your tags are right. We make the tags off the tests."

"OK, so the tags are right off the test, but the test was wrong so that makes the tags wrong. Right?" He gave me an empty stare and I saw us walking into an Abbott and Costello routine. Before he could open his mouth I said, "I'd like to see the non-com in charge."

Out came a sergeant. I made the same explanation, briefer this time, and said, "Sergeant, please do the test again. I'm not going to Vietnam with the wrong blood type on my tags."

The sergeant grunted and disappeared. I waited. A different technician came out studying a piece of paper. He looked up and called my name. He had new tags saying O-positive. Now I was ready for Vietnam, ready to get shot at.

Goodbye

When I left for Vietnam my parents took me to the train station. They had lost a son in a car accident, just nine years old, and now were seeing another son off to combat, not sure they would see him again. Kathleen gave me an embrace with tears in her eyes. I was stupidly cavalier. I gave everyone a quick hug and went down the platform full of empty-headed optimism. Mom told me recently that she turned away crying. She said a woman came up to her, a perfect stranger, patted her on the shoulder and told her it was OK to cry, I would be just fine. Mom did the rest of her crying at home, and there began her long vigil of worry.

VIETNAM

On April 16 at LZ Sherry, gun crewman Jeffrey Lynn Davis dies instantly from massive head injuries incurred in a mortar attack. Two weeks later on April 30, twelve battalions of 8,700 South Vietnamese troops begin an assault into Cambodia. The first attack is aimed at the southern salient of Cambodia protruding into Vietnam known as the Parrot's Beak, 120 miles to the west of LZ Sherry. It is a base area for enemy forces, and a point at which the Ho Chi Minh trail feeds supplies and troops into Vietnam. A U.S. force of 30,000 joins the operation the following day.

LZ Sherry

A Huey helicopter waited on the helipad at LZ Betty outside Phan Thiet. The Huey was the workhorse of the Army, carrying troops, ammunition and supplies to field locations. It was the iconic image of the Vietnam war, pictured taking off with its tail held saucily in the air, seen through a haze of dust with a gunner at the open door. I stepped onto the Huey still thinking of the attack I had seen from the hilltop the night before, and wondered if I was flying to my death.

We lifted to about 500 feet and headed north, away from the sea and toward a low range of mountains. The side doors were open and there was no door gunner on this trip, which opened up a panoramic view of the country as it slid below us. Rice paddies stretched out in a blanket of green patchwork. The sun burst off the surface of the flooded paddies and followed us along our route like a blinking eye. Rivers twisted through the paddies, looping to almost touch themselves. Patches of palm trees appeared as small oases, and plantations showed off their neat rows of rubber trees. As we flew north the Le Hong Fong Forest came into view, a mountainous region of triple canopy jungle. Through it ran the Ho Chi Minh Trail, the north-south supply route of the NVA and VC, carrying troops, munitions, food, equipment and intelligence. The jungle rolled unbroken to the horizon, and beyond our vision it stretched clear into Cambodia. These were the Central Highlands of Vietnam.

LZ Sherry first appeared as a brown smudge in the middle of a vast green checkerboard of rice paddies, like an eraser mark on a beautiful canvas. It sat in the curl of a stream that ran down from the jungle. It was easy at this height to see how the enemy could travel along the banks of the streambed, pop a few mortars or rockets and beat a retreat. Worse yet the streambed was a perfect staging point for ground attacks. LZ Sherry was the bull's eye in a geological shooting gallery. As we approached I saw hundreds of white pockmarks in the earth on either side of the stream, the scars of artillery explosions. An earthen berm and coils of concertina wire defined the perimeter of LZ Sherry. I saw guard towers, machine guns and tracked vehicles that looked like tanks. A circle of howitzers took up one end of the compound, and everywhere there was a confusion of sandbag bunkers, trucks, jeeps and oil drums.

The Huey landed outside the barbed wire, and when I stepped off the helicopter I saw a sign that read like an invitation to tea.

WELCOME TO
LZ SHERRY
HOME OF
'B' BATTERY
5/27 ARTILLERY
BULLS

The lettering was in deep red, the official color of the field artillery. Mortar fins, the remnants of enemy attacks, spelled out LZ SHERRY.

The guys at LZ Sherry reminded me of the troops I saw at Ft. Ord coming out of Vietnam. They went around without shirts or hats, many in boxer shorts or cut-off fatigue pants, tattered at the edges. Some wore flip flops or tennis shoes, while others had boots scuffed to a dusty gray. You could not tell an officer from an enlisted man.

Charlie, a veteran in the Fire Direction Control section, showed me around. We started with the howitzers. There were five of them arranged in a rough cluster toward the west end of the compound. Gun 2 was just outside the FDC bunker, and as we walked into the circle of sandbags protecting the gun I noticed the name BAD NEWS stenciled in white along its barrel. Charlie said, "It's a tradition. Every gun's got a name and it has to start with the letter of the battery." Beside the gun was a low sandbag ammo bunker. I peeked inside and saw shells stacked like cordwood along the walls. In their protective tubes they were the size of a man's leg. They looked bigger here than I remembered from Ft. Sill.

We walked over to Gun 1, named BIRTH CONTROLER. Without thinking I said to Charlie, "It's misspelled."

He turned his head. "Huh?"

"The name. It needs another L."

He looked at the gun. "Looks OK to me."

"It should have two Ls."

"Maybe so, but I'd keep that to myself if I was you."

At Gun 5—BULLWINKLE—two of the gun crew were sitting on a makeshift bench made out of the wood boxes used for shipping artillery shells. Charlie said, louder than he needed to, "Now what you see here are two gun bunnies. They're none too smart, but if you feed them regular and every once in a while give them some gook pussy, they do what they're told."

The one on the left smiled. "Nice to see you too, Charlie. Ever since you went into Fucking Direction Control you don't come around much."

The other one said, "We miss you, Charlie. You did the best 'tube lube' of anybody." And they both laughed.

Charlie said to me, "These are the good ones. The rest of this crew are chained up somewhere."

The one on the left said, "Well Charlie, ain't you gonna introduce us?"

"Meet Specialist 5 Gaydos. He's FDC. Here to whip you guys into shape."

"You a shake 'n' bake?"

I nodded.

"Maybe you can take Charlie's place, make him a gun bunny again. We're short handed here these days."

Charlie turned us around to leave and said over his shoulder, "Stay out from underneath the mortars, fellas." Then he said to me as we walked away, "Everything spelled OK there?"

We walked past BANDIT without stopping. "There was this guy on my old gun, he went home and found out he didn't have a girlfriend anymore. So he's pissed and he runs down to recruiting and re-ups. He's back here and we think he's nuts. Well he's dead now. A mortar got him."

"When?"

"Couple weeks ago. Eight rounds came in that night, all inside the compound. This one blew the shit out of the gun. He was in the ammo bunker but the shrapnel went through the door and found him anyway. Three others wounded." He went quiet and looked at the ground. We were past the last howitzer when he stopped and looked me full in the face. "You want to stay under cover if you can during an attack."

"OK."

"Sounds kind of stupid me telling you that, but guys race for the fins."

"What's the big deal about fins? They're all over the place." Mortar fins sat around by the hundreds, lining shelves and piled in corners. Anyone who wanted a Chinese mortar fin only had to reach out a hand.

"It's a game, to get them when they're still hot. A little advice—you want to collect fins, wait until they stop falling."

He seemed anxious to change the subject. "We get into shirts and hats for the mess hall and formation. Or sometimes there's a shirt alert when some bigshot drops in. But the first couple weeks you need to wear a shirt and a hat when you go outside. It gets pretty warm. I've seen it get up to 130. You get dizzy and want to throw up, you're getting heat stroke. So drink lots of water, even when you're not thirsty. In a couple months you'll get used to it." It sounded like a speech he gave a lot of new guys.

We climbed to the top of an earthen berm that surrounded the battery and looked out on rows of concertina wire coiled like giant springs. There were three rows of concertina, about twenty yards apart. Each row had two coils on the bottom and one on top. Charlie said, "It looks like nothing could get through, especially with the trip flares we got attached every few meters. But a sapper can slip through like shit through a greased horn, even when the little fuckers are loaded down with satchel charges."

"I know. I saw the film. Hard to believe."

"Believe it. If there's incoming you'll hear a siren. If a green flare goes up, there's gooks in the wire. A red goes up they're in the compound raising shit. Whatever, get your flak jacket and steel pot and *di di mau* over to FDC. Don't do anything. Get there and stay out of the way."

I did not say anything.

"Hey, listen. I know you come in country with rank. But it's different over here, really different."

"No, I get it."

"A red flare goes up, you get out of wherever you are unless you want to catch a satchel charge in your lap, or a chicom grenade. Get behind something and stay put. You go running around and you'll get blown away, probably by one of our guys."

Charlie walked down the outside slope of the berm and I followed. He said, "You ever see a claymore mine?" I shook my head. He pointed to a flat rectangle, slightly curved and propped up on its edge. "It's got a load of ball bearings. Makes hamburger out of anybody within a hundred meters. We'll teach you how to set and detonate one without blowing yourself up. See what's written on it?" I looked closer and saw in raised letters FRONT TOWARD ENEMY. "That's the first thing you gotta know."

We walked back to the top of the berm and followed its crest to something that looked like a tank with two barrels. Charlie said, "Forty millimeter cannons. They fire like a pom-pom and put out grenades. When them grenades go off in a row along the ground it looks like an invisible plow—seriously. Everybody calls them Dusters. There's another one over at the other end."

As we continued our tour along the berm a soldier walked

111

by with a blinding white torso and pink arms. Charlie nodded in that direction. "Got here a couple days ago. You cherries are pretty easy to spot. And another thing, for now you don't get an M16 or anything that goes bang. You'll get one after a couple mortar attacks."

"How come?"

"I'll tell you after your first mortar attack, after you've cleaned the shit out of your pants."

We walked a little way and he said, "Some guys like to carry a Thumper instead of a sixteen."

"Thumper?"

"Yeah, a grenade launcher, M79. Looks like a sawed off shotgun. Guys claim they can land a round in mama-san's cleavage. But I don't know. I like the sixteen."

We came to a guard tower and climbed up the ladder. Charlie said, "This here is an M60 machine gun. There's one in every tower. The grunts carry this thing on patrol, one humping the gun and one hauling ammo, both heavy as sin. I don't suppose you know how to shoot one of these. We'll teach you that too. Everybody's got to be able to get on the 60, even the cooks."

I said, "Doesn't look too hard."

"Now it doesn't. But wait till the gooks are coming through the wire. You'll be lucky to aim it in the right direction."

At the north perimeter we looked down on a company of ARVNs, Army of the Republic of South Vietnam. They were bivouacked inside the berm but away from the rest of the battery. They wore full uniforms and looked more military than the Americans. Charlie shook his head. "Worthless bastards. You can dress them up and give them M16s, but they're not

112

good for much. Keep away from them. If we catch one roaming around the battery, we shoot the bastard. Like to anyway. They steal shit like you couldn't believe. And the way they live, the rats follow them everywhere. They're worse than the gooks. Hell, they *are* gooks."

We did not stay long, Charlie did not like even looking at them. Just a few paces along the berm we came to the .50-caliber machine guns. There were four of them mounted on the back of a large truck. Charlie said, "Quad-50s. Here and on the other end, at the south perimeter where the ground attacks come from." A crewman was sitting in the operator's seat with an ammo belt across his chest. The bullets looked like small artillery shells and reached almost from nipple to nipple. I knew something about the .50-caliber because we had fired it at Ft. Sill. The .50-cal was originally an anti-aircraft gun, but brought into ground combat in the early days of Korea to deal with Chinese human wave attacks. When a .50-caliber round hit something, the debris and shrapnel could kill a man within 10 yards. A direct hit could cut him in half. Painted on the rear gate of the truck was *Murder Incorporated*. Charlie saw me looking and said, "All the quad-50s have names. My favorite I saw the other day is *Charlie Chopper*. Get it?"

"I do know how to fire a .50-cal. Not a quad. But I know how to shoot one."

"All we got are quads. Nobody touches them but the crews. They're a nasty piece of business. You're not careful, the barrels heat up and warp, or a round cooks off in the chamber and blows somebody's head off."

We continued around the berm, passed the Duster on the eastern perimeter, and ended at the south end of the compound next to the other quad-50. Charlie said, "You got any questions?"

"Yeah, what happened last night? I saw it from Phan Thi-et."

"Just three or four mortars. They pop them at us every couple of nights. We give back with everything we got. Could be a ground attack, you never know. Besides," he smiled, "it's fun."

"Yeah, it was quite a show."

"Stick around, there'll be more. I don't mean to scare you, but this place can be hell. Half a dozen guys got killed here last year. There was a ground attack too." He pointed off the berm where we were standing. "They came in right there. But we caught 'em in the wire, chewed the shit out of them. Next day they tell me there were body parts hanging everywhere in the wire, including the gook barber that came in to cut hair. 'Head and Shoulders' they called him, because that was all that was left." He looked out over the wire to the surrounding rice paddies. "Most all attacks come from this south side. See that streambed out there? That's how they get close."

"Yeah, I saw it flying in."

He turned around and pointed to one of several small sandbag structures. "That's your hooch right there."

"I don't suppose you have anything on the north side."

"Nope, right here is where all us FDC guys are. Besides, up there is where the ARVNs and all their rats are."

We walked down from the berm to the hooch. It was right beside BIRTH CONTROLER. Charlie said, "You're in here with Mike Leino. He used to be a gun bunny like me." I lowered my head and looked into the dark. I could make out two canvas cots, separated by half a stride. The one on the right had a pillow and a camouflage poncho liner on it. Mine on the left was naked. My back hurt just looking at it.

First Night in the Field

When the sun went down I headed for the FDC bunker. I was too keyed up to sleep and wanted to hang around to see how things worked at night when most of the mortar attacks came. Charlie was there along with two other guys. It was a quiet night so far, and Charlie was still in a talkative mood. "Listen up. At night you have to be ready for anything. There's bound to be mortars and you never know about a ground attack. You wear a steel pot and flak jacket, everywhere. When you get your M16 you carry it everywhere, even to the shitter, right along with your ammo bandolier. You keep a clip locked in, but no round in the chamber. I repeat, *no round in the chamber*. And keep it on SAFE. Takes no time at all to chamber a round and thumb to AUTO or SEMI—no time at all. Applies to everybody. Cooks, gunners, FDC, maintenance, supply, battery commander, lieutenants, sergeants and privates. If I missed anybody it goes for them too. You can wear whatever else you want. Lot of times you got to get places fast, so some of us wear tennis shoes. We don't worry much about how we look, loaded down with stuff and prancing around in white shoes. Looks don't outrun mortars, not that I ever heard of anyway."

"Good advice, but you notice I don't have an M16 yet. I feel kind of naked."

"Maybe you'll get it after tonight, if you don't get yourself blown away. Then you won't be naked anymore."

A guy with a peace symbol around his neck laughed from his chair in the corner. "Yeah, I wouldn't want to share a hooch with no naked guy." Leino lit a cigarette, got up from his chair, and held out his hand. "Pleased to meet you." He had a sleepy, flat look on his face, as if his mind were in a different world. "You can count on Charlie, he's the old man around here."

"I think I may have him by a few years."

"He's still the old man. He was born old."

An explosion went off somewhere outside and I jumped. Charlie said, "It's just H&I. You'll get used to it. After awhile you won't even hear it."

"What the hell is H&I?"

"I'll explain it." He used a teacher's tone as if talking to a child. "The Viet Cong and North Vietnamese Army like to sneak up on us, and we don't like that they should do that. So every night one gun shoots off a high explosive round every so often to keep the little bastards from hanging around too long. It's called harassment and interdiction." After a dramatic pause he added, "I don't know how to spell it, but that's what it is."

A voice came from around the corner, "I think I know." Its owner walked into the room carrying a guitar by its neck, and also wearing a peace symbol. *Were these things Army issue?*

"It's OK," Charlie said. "Meet one of our new guys. It's his first day at Sherry." Charlie turned to me, "Fred is our other resident hippy. He spends most of his time in a little back room playing with himself…sorry, playing *to* himself."

116

Fred gave me a wide, innocent smile. I said, "Hi. Nice guitar."

"I didn't think it was allowed, but I sent home for it anyway. It just got here."

Another explosion went off. I jumped again and everybody laughed. I said, "That was a lot louder." Then I heard a "pop" and the door of the bunker lit up as if it were daylight.

"Illumination round," Charlie said. "The gun's right outside the door. It'll go on all night too."

I had seen BULLWINKLE on my way to FDC with its tube pointed almost straight up. The sun was going down and at a certain angle the big red ball sat on the very tip of the howitzer's muzzle. It reminded me of a giant cherry lollipop.

"When the illumination gun raises its tube," Charlie said, "that's the signal for the guards to start their tower shifts. At night it's the most important job on the firebase. Anything could mean gooks, like for instance a shadow or a funny noise that don't sound natural. You got to be paying attention. All the fancy equipment they send out here isn't worth much compared to a good guard. We got night vision binoculars, but they make your eyes hurt after a couple minutes, like they're going to roll out of your skull. There's two radar units for picking up movement, and they sent us these things you stick in the ground that are supposed to feel people walking around. I wish I had a nickel for every water buffalo we probably blew away. None of it's worth a shit when it's raining, which you'll see is damn near every night during monsoon. Any day give me a guy in the tower that's not asleep and knows what he's listening for.

"A mortar makes this hollow sound you can hear a ways off." Charlie rounded his mouth and stuck the tip of his tongue out just a little past his teeth. "*Thoomp*. It's pretty loud and sometimes you can hear it inside your hooch. A good guard's on the line to FDC before it lands, and a really good one knows where it's coming from. We get lucky, radar will pick it up too, but that doesn't happen all the time. FDC hits the siren and now everybody knows there's incoming, if they didn't already know. Ground attacks always start with mortars. So everybody gets on their piece and blows the shit out of their field of fire. I'm talking quad-50s, Dusters, all the guns except the one on illumination. So do the guys in the towers with their machine guns. Plenty of fireworks. Any gooks out there are going to be hamburger, like last year."

"What do we do while all this is going on?"

Leino said. "If they get through the wire, bend over and kiss your butt goodbye."

"What else?" The wise cracks were beginning to wear thin on me.

Charlie said, "Mostly they throw two or three mortars at us, sometimes six or eight, then haul ass. We get a pretty good idea of where the mortars are coming from, and they know we know, somewhere along the streambed usually. So here's what we do, we figure up firing data for that spot and blow the shit out of it. A couple high explosive rounds going off in the air to get any gooks hiding behind the bank. But likely they're gone by then. If they hit us again that night it's always from another spot.

"Gooks aren't stupid. But they're lousy shots. No telling where them things are going to land. Might hit a hooch, or blow out some truck tires. I seen them go clear over and land outside the wire. But I seen them land near a gun too and mess guys up. I'm talking about Viet Cong, the local guys in black pajamas and sandals. Now the North Vietnamese Army is another thing

118

entirely. They're more like regular army, trained and tough. They got rockets and can put one in your left ear if they want. Mean mothers, them rockets. Go right through a hooch wall on a bad day. No, you don't want to fuck with the NVA, not unless you got the 101st airborne and the 50th infantry on your side, plus a couple Cobra gunships."

"Any ground attacks lately?"

"Nope. We got a reputation for being hard to overrun. We got a small perimeter and lots of firepower. They learned their lesson last year, but every so often they test the wire, sneak a few gooks up close before a mortar attack. But I tell you, that's dangerous duty.

"Then again there's nights when nothing happens. Get's fearful boring. You can write letters or read books, they come free. The cigarettes are free too, but they don't help much with the time. You get to cross off the day at midnight, but that don't take any time either. You can do anything but sleep. Lot of guys play cards. Some shake 'n' bake started up a Bridge game. Which I don't know much about, but only four can play so it can't be much of a game. Come morning, you feel good you made it through another night in the Nam. If you want they let you volunteer for tomorrow too.

"I'll tell you what else we do. Every night at about this time we plot the night positions of all the friendlies out there. There's a lot of them: U.S., ARVN, Korean, Aussies, even sometimes Canadian. Don't want to accidently blow up our buddies." Fred began reading map coordinates and unit designations off a piece of paper, while Charlie and Leino stuck pins in two large map boards in the center of the room.

I went back to my hooch to try to get some sleep. I put my helmet and flack jacket beside the cot, rolled up my fatigue

119

jacket for a pillow, and folded my blanket into a makeshift mattress. It was stifling inside the hooch. I stripped down to my boxers and just as I was laying down an explosion erupted, close enough to shake the hooch and light the doorway. I jumped up and heard another explosion, but further away, that sent a tremor through the ground. Was this a mortar attack? But there was no siren, no machine guns. I peaked outside around the flak wall that protected the opening to the hooch. All was quiet. I saw three crewmembers on the howitzer next to my hooch loading a shell. BIRTH CONTROLER was shooting H&I that night, just my luck. I did not remember a howitzer being that loud, but I had never been this close to the muzzle when it fired.

I went back to bed, only to be rocked by another blast as I tried to push myself to sleep. It fired every twenty minutes or so, followed by the impact of the rounds. Sometimes the fire went directly over my hooch. The muzzle flash lit the doorway and shook a dusting of sand from the ceiling. I could hear the whizz of the shell going overhead. There were other blasts, followed by a loud pop: BAD NEWS beside FDC shooting illumination. With these the hooch opening glowed for a couple minutes and melted to black again. I lay awake trying to sort out the sounds and listening for a *thoomp*.

With the first glow of daylight I stepped out of my hooch in a shirt and hat as required. It was already hot. I heard a familiar sound I could not place right away. Then I knew. It was the sound of an AK47, the automatic rifle used by the NVA and VC. I recognized its sharp popping sound from training tapes. I turned back into the hooch, sat on my cot and waited. There was more gunfire, automatic rifles and machine guns. Real bullets. I felt a wave of nausea. They wanted to kill me.

120

The thought gripped my chest and made it ache—*someone was out to take my life.* In that defining instant my whole world changed; I changed. I forgot the values of my upbringing about the sanctity of life. I overthrew years of priestly formation aimed at helping other people. In a blink I was ready to kill. Before he killed me. It was oh-so easy, no more bother than putting on a different hat.

When the noise quieted down I ventured outside again, this time in my steel pot and flack jacket, only to see the battery going about its daily business. Leino was just coming back from his night shift. He said, "What are you all dressed up for?"

"I heard the shooting,"

He laughed. "That was our sniper, if you can call him that. He can't hit a barn. He's our breakfast entertainment every few weeks. Throws a few rounds in our direction and then it's *di di mau,* he takes off." Leino flicked his hand in the air, "He ain't much of a sniper."

"All the shooting…"

"Our guys having some fun with him." He walked into our hooch saying, "You can take off the gear, you're safe now."

But I did not feel safe, and despite the incompetent sniper, despite the silliness of the event, I had stepped across a line as profound as any in my life, a line that could not be uncrossed. It was not a choice, but a simple acceptance to destroy whoever I needed to destroy to stay alive. That instant marked my true arrival in Vietnam, a momentous moment wrapped inside a joke.

The Battle of LZ Betty

I was sleeping in my hooch when the mortar landed. Then another. There was no mistaking the sharp crack of the explosion and the hammer blow to the ground. The attack siren went off and now there were more explosions and machine guns. I put on my helmet and flak jacket and started out for FDC. I stopped in the doorway and looked out on a scene I had only imagined. Illumination flares hung in the sky and a haze of black smoke drifted in the air. Figures ran in all directions, materializing from the shadows and disappearing. There was a metallic smell of gunpowder and everywhere a mayhem of explosions, shouting and machine guns. Every instinct told me to stay in my hooch. I would die two steps out the door. Still I left the hooch and started running. BIRTH CONTROLER was roaring and belching fire as I passed it. I had to put my fingers in my ears as I ran. An illumination flare popped, showing other running bodies and men busy about their howitzers.

Inside the FDC bunker I went to a corner. The place was packed with bodies and gear. Everybody was shouting, two guys screaming into radio mics and another on the landline handset with a finger in his other ear. Two guys crowded each other on a map board, figuring gun data against the mortar sites. Then we were taking incoming AK47 sniper fire, and the guys on the chart jumped to figuring return howitzer fire for that too. Now word came that our sister battery at LZ Betty outside Phan Thiet was under a ground attack. It needed artillery. Two bodies hopped to the other map board to plot targets and calculate gun commands. The fire direction officer pulled four guns for the mission, keeping one on illumination and leaving the perimeter to the machine guns and Dusters. He called for HE rounds and gave the *fire for effect* command, telling the guns to fire as fast as they could until told to stop. There was no need for smoke or adjustments because we were aiming at fixed defensive targets which had already been plotted and registered on Betty's perimeter. The howitzers roared in unison, sending out volley after volley, half a ton of explosives.

Mortars started falling on us again, louder and sharper over the howitzers and shaking the ground. I heard machine guns and Duster cannons open up again, raking the perimeter against a possible ground attack.

The action stopped a little after 3:00 a.m. We had no casualties that night, but LZ Betty was not so fortunate. In the morning we learned that she had taken heavy casualties. An NVA infantry battalion of five companies in consort with five companies of VC, a force of about 350, had attacked LZ Betty. They killed seven U.S. soldiers and wounded thirty-five, leaving behind fourteen bodies of their own they could not carry off. That night 130 attacks occurred against firebases and installations in the region. LZ Betty was the only one to suffer a ground attack.

The attack on LZ Betty and other installations through-out the Central Highlands never made it into U.S. newspapers. The next day on May 4, 1970 at Kent State University in Ohio, National Guardsmen shot and killed four student protesters and wounded nine. In response to the killings, over 400 colleges and universities across America shut down. In Washington, nearly 100,000 protesters surrounded government buildings, including the White House. The news of fighting in Vietnam was pushed for the moment from national attention.

The story that eventually emerged of the Battle of LZ Betty tells a tale of a military installation that was ripe for the taking. Cavernous erosion ditches ran from the edge of the plateau on its eastern perimeter down to the sea, making the ditches prime avenues for enemy infiltration. Requests to have them filled had gone unheeded. Even the rules at LZ Betty played into the hands of the enemy. Perimeter guards could not fire on the enemy without permission from the officer of the day. The OD had to see and identify the enemy before he could let anyone open fire. A sighting by the perimeter guard was not enough. In a further effort to avoid accidental engagement, all M16s, grenade launchers and machine guns—even .45 pistols—were locked away in the maintenance bunker. That included the personal weapons of Company B, 1/50 mechanized infantry just returned from action in the field. Getting them back required clearance, and then each weapon had to be released by serial number and signed for.

A forward observer team from LZ Sherry attached to Company B, Sergeant Pierce and radio operator Bill Wright, were at Betty the night of May 3, 1970. They, and the other men who were there that night, tell the full story of what happened. The attack began at 1:45 in the morning.

Bryan (Frenchy) Lagimoniere:

Due to the My Lai Massacre then hitting the States, we were told you could only shoot if you were authorized by the Officer of the Day. Tower 7 reported sappers in the wire and the guys called for permission to open fire, but the OD said, "No!" He came out to Tower 7, and had apparently been drinking. He looked out and couldn't see the sappers in the wire, so he wouldn't allow any firing. After the OD got into his jeep and drove off two mortar rounds hit where his jeep had been.

I had my radio on and just as the DJ said, "Good morning Vietnam, it's now 1:45 a.m..." the first mortar hit. It was Sunday. As the mortar rounds fell we were pinned down in our tent. Two sappers went by and one dropped a homemade grenade in my lap that failed to go off.

And one minute later I was hit with a Chi-com (Chinese Communist) grenade in my flak jacket that also failed to go off. And to make the night even more fun a mortar round went off just in front of me knocking me unconscious for about a minute. The shit house behind us was hit, graves registration was hit, they leveled the orderly room, our tent was riddled with small arms fire and the supply hooch across from us was hit and the list goes on.

I remember hearing Randy scream as our jeep was hit and we went airborne and landed inside a bunker. Buchanan was nowhere to be seen. I had to lay still and play possum until the gooks, who were running all over me, were forced out of the LZ after a couple hours, seemed like forever. I just prayed, cried and shit. I had lost my M16 and rounds were landing everywhere. When an illumination flare would pop, I could see the VC dragging their wounded and dead through the wire towards the cemetery. I had a perfect view, just no weapon.

Chuck Nelson, Supply Sergeant:

Yes, I was at LZ Betty when all the weapons were locked up. It was ordered and man was I just as mad as all the guys when we were attacked that night. I didn't pay attention to serial numbers when issuing the weapons that night as each person came to me for one. It was a crazy idea and I hope that no one was killed because of it.

Gus Allbritton:

The buildings were on fire, the choppers had been satchel-charged and sappers had thrown charges into every hooch and bunker that wasn't defended.

Bill (Little Bill) Wright, B Battery, 5th Battalion, 27th Field Artillery (LZ Sherry):

I remember May 3 about as well as most guys that are scared almost out of their minds. When the first attack hit the towers and the wire areas my FO Sergeant Pierce and myself

126

*were at the artillery command bunker. Pierce
and I grabbed our weapons and headed out
for the Duster bunker to the right of Tower 3.
We never made it. We ran head first into a full
blown firefight just about thirty meters short of
our objective. Pierce took a round in the upper
leg which made him fall over backwards into
me. I was not about to leave him there by himself. I managed to get him and myself behind
some sand bags and propped him up so that
he was able to fire his weapon in one direction
while I sat with my back to his and covered the
other direction. We seemed to be holding our
own when everything turned to shit. From this
point I don't remember a lot. I do remember
that about five or six guys from the 1/50 pulled
our fat out of the fire. Which was about the
time I took two rounds, one in the back right
side and the other in the right upper leg. I must
have passed out because when I woke up I was
in Phan Rang and Pierce was in the bed next
to me.*

Ray Lack, Maintenance Platoon:

*It has been very difficult for me to read the
"memories" of 3 May 1970 through my tears. I
lost a great deal of my memory after getting hit
but I remember very well men lined up at the
supply hooch drawing weapons while all hell
was breaking loose all around us. I was with
the maintenance platoon, and we had refused
to turn in our weapons as ordered. I was very
short (soon to leave Vietnam) by that time and*

getting very anxious. When the satchel charges started going off all over we jumped into a 3/4 ton truck and headed for the perimeter. We took what I thought was a rocket in front and bailed out onto the road. Robert Haney was next to me when he was blown up. There were "gooks" coming in human waves as far as you could see in every direction. I couldn't understand why we weren't blowing the claymores so I crawled up on a nearby bunker to blow them just as a flare lit up the top of the bunker. There were gooks on top and they immediately opened up with AK's. I stopped a number of rounds with my flak jacket and the impact threw me off the bunker backwards. I hit the ground firing and within a second or maybe two, four mortar rounds landed within a few feet of me. One severed my right leg. I was pretty messed up but still remember the NVA standing next to me firing at our guys. Every time he fired his expended cartridges landed on my exposed skin and burned. I wouldn't be here if it wasn't for a black man, possibly a medic, who took out the NVA soldier next to me. He threw me over his shoulder, handed me my leg and ran for what seemed like forever to a jeep. He took me to the base infirmary where they took one look and tagged me for Medevac.

Dave Hess:

I was so upset about the attack that I wrote my congressman. A formal letter was sent to the unit requiring the brass to answer why our weapons were locked up. Captain Carl Abbot

*called me into his office and showed me his re-
sponse to the request. He told my congressman
that the attack wasn't that bad and that I was
just young and scared. I still have the letter
and hope someday to meet Abbot.*

Captain Ray Sarlin, recent commander of Company C,
1/50, which was then still in the field:

*When the attack started, I threw on my clothes
and gear and scrambled to the TOC (Tactical
Operations Center) to see what was happen-
ing. I felt naked without an M16, especially
since just hours before I was commanding a
mechanized infantry company in the field.*

*As the longest serving officer in the battalion...
I was asked to identify the bodies from that
night. Each body was laid out on a separate
table in a row of tables in a tent. The mind
plays tricks, but for years I distinctly remembered examining bodies on seven tables but
the records only list six men killed. It wasn't
easy identifying the bodies of the men whom I
knew—one head was missing—but I was able
to positively identify all the bodies except one
by appearance or some distinguishing feature.
For example, the headless man had written his
name on his jungle boots.*

*The following night, early on the morning of
May 4, the compound at LZ Betty was attacked
again. Events began at 3:55 a.m. with a ra-*

dar sighting of potential enemy activity off the western perimeter, the same direction of the attack the previous night. Alpha battery, located at that end of the compound, dumped thirty-three rounds on the grid supplied by the radar unit. Three minutes later a B-40 rocket from that direction struck between bunkers 8 and 9, immediately in front of Alpha Battery. Alpha responded with another thirty-three rounds on the suspected location. Thirteen minutes later at 4:11 a.m., bunker 9 spotted a VC at 100 yards and cut him down with .50-cal machine gun fire, the rules for getting permission to fire apparently suspended. Nineteen minutes later at 4:30 a.m. bunkers 8 and 9 began taking small arms fire. They spotted a VC inside the barbed wire running along the airstrip toward their bunkers. They lost sight of him and held their fire. But Alpha battery saturated the perimeter with twelve rounds. Just before dawn bunker 9 heard a metallic sound, perhaps of wire being cut. That ended a tense night for LZ Betty, no friendly casualties and one possible enemy KIA. No body was recovered.

Note: Quotes from the men at LZ Betty and the above description of the Kent State shootings reprinted from the 1st Bn (Mech) 50th Infantry website http://www.ichiban1.org/.

Armed and Dangerous

The next day Charlie said to me, "Well, your cherry got popped last night. Get over to supply and get your M16. And try not to get lost."

Anxious to get my weaponry, I double-timed to the supply bunker and said to the clerk, "First give me a Thumper to play with before I decide."

"You sure?"

"Why wouldn't I be?"

"All those grenades strapped across your chest and piled up in your hooch? That'd make me nervous. And they load one at a time. I get in a spot I want automatic. Nothin beats the 16."

I took the Thumper and a bandolier of grenade rounds out to the berm. The grenades looked like fat shotgun shells. The Thumper was a break-action piece with a short, fat barrel, like an overweight sawed-off shotgun. It did not take long to get the knack for lobbing a round close to a target, feeling the satisfying thump it gave to the ground. But the clerk was right. I could not imagine I wanted it in a fight. Back at the supply hooch I said to the clerk, "I'll take the 16."

"I thought you would. You know officers and non-coms get a .45 if you want one. Most of them do, but they never use them for anything."

"You bet I want one."

The .45 came into use during WWI and saw wide service in WWII and Korea. The Vietnam model still had the classic lines and heft of the original. The .45 was fun to carry holstered on the hip, western style. In the hand it was a functioning piece of history, but not much of a fighting weapon, it was accurate to only thirty yards and gave a tremendous kick. I only wore the .45 on convoys into Phan Thiet, more as a fashion accessory than a weapon. When I strapped it to my hip I felt like Randolph Scott, my boyhood cowboy hero.

Fire Direction Control

Everything worth knowing went through the FDC bunker. It was the combat, intelligence, operations and psychiatric center of the battery. Corner to corner it was packed with gear: three radios, two large map tables, slide rulers, protractors, target grids, plotting scales, charts and manuals. Covering the walls were radio call signs, ammo inventories and diagrams. The most consulted wall decoration was the battery calendar with bold red Xs over the days safely passed, each drawn at midnight by the night crew.

The place was overwhelming the first time I walked in and looked around. I had forgotten half of what I had learned in training, and the half I remembered was not relevant in Vietnam. Mike Leino was on the radio. Listening to him made me sick. He said, "Copy Firefox eight niner, we got ears, meet you up a dime." He fiddled with the dial and said, "Rocks two five November Echo. Hold." He squelched the handset, which seemed to mean something. "Delta November Papa through Titty. Alpha November eight four five...six niner seven."

Another radio came to life. From its speaker came, "Yankee South this is High Flyer, I got elephant nuts."

Mike said, "Hold" into the first radio and gave another squelch on the handset. Into the second radio he said, "High Flyer, you are good to go in one zero at Sierra Sierra." He gave two squelches on the handset and returned to the first radio, "Rocks confirmed, but that's a big negative on the little people. I hear they're going to *di di mau*. Nothing yet through Titty." Two squelches. He picked up the landline phone. "Junk, elephant nuts with juice in one zero."

I heard the double rotor of a Chinook helicopter and went outside to look. It hovered outside the wire with two big rubber bladders dangling from its underside. Elephant nuts. They were 500-gallon blivets of diesel fuel. Juice. In this way I learned my job all over again, one word and one phrase at a time.

When someone might be listening in on the radio, the operator chose another frequency up or down the dial. A dime bought ten kilohertz. "Rocks" were ROKs, Republic of Korea soldiers notorious for not telling anyone where they were bivouacked for the night. But that information was often available through the relay station at Whiskey Mountain, shaped like breasts and known as Titty Mountain. The little people were South Vietnamese infantry and when they moved quickly it was always *di di mau*. Saying "over" and "over and out" was a waste of breath when a squelch or two on the handset would do. Charlie was right. This was really different.

First Letter

I wrote it under a flashlight.

I know you are all anxious to hear about LZ Sherry, the firing battery that will be my home for the next few months. Well, the food is good; much better than anything the Army ever served up in the states. But most of all I suppose you want to know how safe it is here. I'm not going to tell you it's like being in my mother's arms. It isn't. We take sniper fire and of course mortar rounds every so often, just like every other firebase in Vietnam. And there is always the danger of the gooks getting through our perimeter. BUT - here's the

good part. We are also the fin-
est battery in the whole 1st Field
Force – the best defended against
attack and the most accurate.
We've always got brass out here
touring the place.

I work an "8 on – 8 off" shift
around the clock, which means
I spend most of my time working or sleeping. I'm still very
skittery, especially at night when
the VC does all its work. During our first mortar attack I
just about wet my pants. I still
have to distinguish between our
own weapons firing and what is
incoming. When one of those
howitzers fires it sounds like
the world is coming to an end.
And we have so many different
types of weapons that it will
take me some time to identify
them by sound. Meanwhile I will
be jumping out of my drawers.

Let me end as optimistically as
I can. I've got it better than
a lot of guys over here and I'm
working with some pretty com-
petent people.

First Kill

I was itching for the fight after the battle of LZ Betty, and there was plenty to get into. Two nights after Betty we began taking small arms fire from the southeast. A platoon of the 1/50 Mechanized had set up for the night in that area and returned fire for us. We held our own fire for fear of involving their position. They silenced the enemy with their .50-caliber machine gun, but in the process a round cooked off in the chamber, exploding the gun and wounding its crewman.

Later that night, a few minutes after midnight, we got a call from an ARVN infantry unit, South Vietnamese regular army, under attack by the VC. The guys in FDC were relieved when the call came for just illumination rounds. Shooting high explosive for the ARVN made us nervous because we were never sure exactly where the rounds were landing. In all the battery put up twenty-seven illumination rounds. Two ARVN were killed and two wounded in the engagement. They did manage to capture an M16 from the VC. This was my first exposure to the fact that the VC possessed a substantial number of M16s and M79 grenade launchers.

One afternoon, with two weeks to my credit at Sherry, an inbound helicopter spotted three VC, who promptly opened fire on the aircraft and then took off. We chased them with three smoke rounds and when we thought they had come to ground fired off three HE. A platoon of the 1/50 made a sweep of the area and called in another forty rounds on the suspected location. Nothing came of it, but we hoped the show of firepower would discourage future bad behavior. Not so. The following morning another helicopter belonging to the 1/50 took on ground fire departing from Sherry. This was a combat assault chopper used to being shot at and continued on its journey.

Several nights later at exactly the stroke of midnight, we came under a mortar attack. Five landed inside the battery. The guard tower picked up the location and we opened up on it with everything we had. The ordinance report the next morning recorded the we expended twenty HE artillery rounds, over 400 Duster grenades and close to 4000 .50-cal machine gun rounds. With no casualties and no material damage, this was a "good" mortar attack.

At 9:55 in the morning two days later, a sniper opened fire on us. This must have been an intelligent sniper, because he was 300 yards out, a distance just inside the effective range of an AK47 but relatively safe. The Dusters threw out a handful of grenades and quieted him down. Half an hour later he opened up again on an approaching helicopter and drew more Duster retaliation. This game went on all morning, him popping up to harass passing helicopters, then ducking into his hole before a Duster grenade found him. We decided not to waste any artillery rounds on him. The Dusters were having fun, so we let them have it to themselves. There were no casualties and no damages. It was a "good" sniper attack.

First Kill

Two weeks later at midnight an ARVN unit engaged with a VC platoon just off its night defensive perimeter. They were taking AK47 and rocket fire. Fortunately, earlier in the evening according to protocol we had plotted all friendly positions in our sector. This allowed us to get rounds in the air in a couple minutes, thirty rounds in all. The official after action report credited B Battery with four enemy KIA. My first kills.

Top

Make no mistake, First Sergeant Stolberg ran LZ Sherry. The officers played their parts, but the first sergeant pulled the strings. He went by Top. He had spent his adult life engaged in warfare—WWII, Korea and now a second tour in Vietnam. Top was old school artillery, and half deaf because earplugs were for pussies. He knew more about artillery than the rest of the battery combined, and had seen battles we only read about in school. Top's combat career showed in his face. It looked like tire tread. And he did not take guff from anybody.

The more I got to know Top the less I liked him. He had a temper, charming one minute and shouting the next. I never knew what would set him off. From halfway across the battery I could tell what kind of a mood he was in by the shade of his face.

Every morning Top called a formation. He held it at different locations around the battery, to keep the VC guessing. Placing soldiers in the same spot at the same time every day was asking for trouble. Top's formations were quick and all business. He was keen on haircuts, upcoming inspections, work details, and the sorry state of the sad sacks under his command. Sometimes he pulled out a sheet of paper with a new policy from the Pentagon or battalion headquarters and read it word-for-word, not hiding his contempt for directives that had little to do with fighting the war.

Top's main concern at formation was everybody's where-abouts. He had to keep track of a gang of young men confined to a one-acre firebase like caged monkeys. Most were teenagers and all had guns. At the daily formation when the section chief said, "All present," Top looked up and down the rank. They had better have all been there.

If the chief added, "...or accounted for," Top turned a red face in his direction and shouted, "So where the fuck are they? What are they doing that is so God-awful more important than my formation?"

Sometimes a section chief said, "One absent, First Sergeant." This was shorthand for, *I am missing a man and I have no idea where he is.* Top's eyes would turn to blue marbles and he would say in a low voice, "You go find him right now. I'll see both of you in my hooch at ten hundred hours."

It was not so, but it seemed like everybody sooner or later got gonorrhea. Some guys made a hobby of it. On a trip to Phan Thiet I was walking down a side street with a guy from Sherry. Vendors waved us over and mama-sans pulled at our sleeves, "Come see top notch girl." My companion could not resist. Before following the mama-san he took off his wedding ring. "I always take the ring off," he said. "Then it don't mean nothin'."

Five days after convoys to Phan Thiet—I could count them—soldiers lined up outside Top's hooch begging for a medical pass. They held their crotches while Top yelled at them. Then at formation he yelled at everybody. "You come back with the clap, you'll never see the rear again the rest of your goddamn tour. Tell you what, I'm going to start giving Article 15s for damaging Army property. Your dick belongs to Uncle Sam, you hear me? You can play with it all you want, but you bring it back dripping, I'll have your ass."

Top invited the battalion surgeon out to give us a talk on the ravages of venereal disease in Vietnam. The doctor said that one strain had no cure. Top added, "In other words, you go to Japan and wait for your dick to rot off." But the gonorrhea kept on, taking heavy casualties after every convoy.

Formation on this day was next to Gun 2. We fell in at ease while Top stood with his hands behind his back. We knew something important was coming when Top skipped the section chief reports. He got straight to the point. "Every time one of you goes to Phan Thiet you come back with a sore dick. So I give you a pass to get a shot in your ass. In a month you come back holding it in your hand again and crying for another pass. Well I'm sick of it. Goddamn fucking sick of it. So I'm going to help you out."

Top reached into his pocket with his left hand and pulled out something small and square. "A lot of you have never seen one of these. It's called a condom. When I was a kid we called 'em rubbers." He smiled, but in a wicked sort of way. "And for you momma's boys who don't know how to use one, I'm gonna show you right now. Pay attention."

Top pulled his right hand from behind his back and held up a broom. He held it in the middle of the handle. "This is you." Guys elbowed each other and pointed to the broom handle. Top thought a moment, "Well maybe this ain't exactly you." He slid his hand up to near the end. "Is that more like it?" Everyone looked at somebody else. More elbowing, some laughing.

He slipped the broom under his armpit, and went to open the condom. He struggled with it, ignoring the free advice coming from the formation. Finally he bit the corner and got the rubbery thing out in the open. He then sent it into battle. He showed the tactical positioning on the tip of the broom handle. He demonstrated the maneuver of unrolling it. When he came to the last step he said, "You can't pull this thing on like a sock. You got to leave some room at the end." He snapped the little empty hat at the end of the condom. "It ain't pretty, but neither are you."

The back row fell down laughing, starting at one end and going like a wave to the other. Some guys rolled on the ground holding their stomachs. The boy beside me bent over with his hands on his knees, having a hard time breathing. A guy walked away waving his arms, came back, went away and then back again, not sure where he wanted to be. Guys started punching each other on the shoulder.

"Settle down," Top yelled. "I got a whole case of these in my hooch. You come in and get a handful before going to the rear. They're free. No excuses. You come back with the clap, I'm not shittin' I'll cut the goddamn thing off."

Not long after this I was at the latrine and could hardly stand for the burning. *Oh boy*, I thought. I went to Top and told him I needed to get to the hospital. "I don't know how this happened, Top. Honest to God I never put my toe in the water."

He looked at me. "It's not your toe we're talking about."

I went to the regimental hospital in Phan Rang, where the medics took a culture, gave me a bag of pills and told me to come back in two days. The technician said, "You got a whole zoo growing in there." He said it was nonspecific urethritis, from highly unsanitary conditions. *VD without the fun*,

I thought. Vietnam found a way to screw everybody. I never told Top about getting the clap without sex. It felt like trying to explain how a virgin gets pregnant. But I made sure it never happened again. I started washing my hands *before* going to the latrine.

The Humble Sandbag

Like all wars throughout history, Vietnam was fought as much with a shovel as a rifle. Of all the activities needed to maintain a firebase, sandbags took up the most time—filling them, laying them into walls, and then tearing them out of old structures. Sandbags by the tens of thousands went into flak walls, hooches, ammo bunkers and guard towers. They were olive drab like everything else in the battery: the howitzers, machine guns, trucks, generators, oil drums, flashlights, food containers, uniforms, even the olive drab condom that Top deployed on his broomstick. "I'm starting to piss OD," one soldier said. Sandbags were mundane things, until they stopped a bullet or grabbed a piece of shrapnel. Torn, tattered and scorched they became things of beauty.

There was no end to building new hooches and fixing ones that were either falling down or rotting down. I was at Sherry less than two weeks when I wrote:

I filled sandbags all day. We're rebuilding the hooches where the FDC guys stay before the monsoon season. Four of us worked all day and only got the roof finished.

My first time in the sand pit my partner and I put on a small comedy. With a full shovel of sand I went for the bag my partner held open, while he moved the bag to chase the shovel. It was a battle of wills between the shovel and the bag.

"Hold still," I said.

"No, you hold still."

Our first attempt at building a hooch resulted in walls made of half-filled bags with loose ends peeking out. The next day there were rivulets of sand running down its sides. When the monsoon rains came a few months later, the hooch melted a little with each downpour.

After a few hundred sandbags I learned the fine points of the job: the exact amount of sand to scoop onto the shovel, the precise angle to slip the load into the bag, and the rhythmic efficiency of delivering four shovels of sand to a bag without pausing. When building a wall I learned that there had to be a precise amount of sand in the bag, that it had to be tamped down, and that the ends had to be folded under to prevent leaking. I learned how to lay the bags like bricks, tapering the walls inward for stability. I took some pride that I could make the walls meet at their corners in a neat finger weave pattern, possible only if the bags were of uniform size to begin with. The only person better than me was Charlie. Nobody beat Charlie.

I came to love construction duty because it got me out of the FDC cave and its endless stream of military paperwork. This was real work out in the sun where I belonged. I had adjusted quickly to the heat in Vietnam and my skin was now crayon-brown. I could fill sandbags all day without raising a sweat. Then it was the cold that bothered me. I needed a jacket for anything below ninety degrees. Perhaps it was the Bedouin in me coming out, happy in his world of sand and sun.

Curly

We all arrived at LZ Sherry on the same day, three *shake
'n' bakes* with formal training in fire direction control. Kent
Nygaard had a sober, kind face and was always ready for serious conversation. He and I had long talks about surviving
the craziness of Vietnam during our night shifts together. He
thought deeply about the war and our involvement, and when
he said, *I've been thinking,* we were in for a long talk.

Jim Jenkins carried a toothpick between his teeth and
talked in the warm liquid way of a southern boy. He was quick
with a smile and had a little chuckle for almost any topic. Greg
had the annoying habit of leaping to practical solutions while
Kent and I were just beginning to discuss the options.

Top had to pick one of us as section chief. He picked Jim,
sending Kent and me into the ranks as shift leaders. Jim was
younger than us and had no college education. I chose to believe that is why Top picked him, out of some old Army bias
against college graduates, even though I knew Jim had more
time in country and possessed seniority, which made it an easy
decision for Top. I resented Jim and questioned every decision.

He put us on a crazy schedule of eight-on-eight-off, and when that proved disastrous he went to twelve-on-twelve-off, switching shifts every two weeks. Just when you were getting used to nights you went on days, and then back to nights again. Jim seemed to be experimenting his way into the job. After Jim took over nobody was happy.

Curly, the section chief when we arrived, was the biggest loser under this new arrangement. He had been running a good FDC, but now he had to train and simultaneously take orders from three cherries, who together knew a fraction of what he did about the job. Curly had been kicked out of Officer Candidacy School a few days before graduation over a minor infraction, and then packed off to Vietnam. He held a special contempt for the military and all of its representatives. The new *shake 'n' bakes* added another measure of bitterness to his outlook.

Curly and I had a rough beginning. For the first few weeks we circled like two dogs spoiling for a fight. When he was not complaining or finding fault, he sat in a silent funk. I thought, *If he wants to act like a child, I'll treat him like a child.* I took on the tone of an adult watching over an irresponsible child. "Curly, don't forget the ammo report needs to be out by 0900."

"No it doesn't. That's when we hear from the guns what they shot during the night. The battalion report goes in at noon. But OK, fine. Just don't come back to me when it fucks up." Which of course it did.

Curly and I were too much alike: full of ourselves, unhappy and stuck in a mutual death grip.

I often retreated into an abandoned guard tower to get away. It was the only place I found some peace. I did not think about anything there. I just stared at the sky. During the dry season the sun came off the dust in the air and made a floating tapestry of red and purple. One evening I sat content, lost in another sunset, when a thought came. *Show him that you like him.* I was not even thinking of Curly at the time. I said to myself, *Give in? Kiss his behind? Pretend I like him when I don't?* I do not know who answered, but whoever it was said *Yes!*

I had to stew over it for a few days. One evening I asked him if he wanted to play cribbage. It felt like poking a hornet's nest. In a casual tone he said, "Sure." The next night we played again, and it became a habit.

One evening I ventured into a real conversation. "You know, Curly, I really shouldn't be here. I was in the seminary. Had an automatic deferment. Left and got my ass drafted. Talk about stupid."

"Maybe. I don't suppose you got any pussy there."

"About as much as I'm getting here. It was kind of frowned on."

"Giving up a deferment." He shook his head.

"So what bright thing got you kicked out of OCS?"

"I still can't hardly believe it." He was quiet for a while. "The week before graduation, after twenty-five weeks, six of us went to get our uniforms from the cleaners. I signed out and so did two others. Three didn't bother to sign out at all. Well, it took more time than we thought it would and when we got back they said we went places besides the cleaners, which wasn't what happened at all. Still they said we signed out fraudulently and kicked all three of us out."

"Did you get a trial or anything?"

"Nope. That's not how they did things. But what really burns me is the three guys who didn't sign out at all got to graduate, got their commissions."

"Any chance they had too many second lieutenants and

were just looking for an excuse to kick guys out?"

"Maybe. I don't know. Never thought about it."

"Or send some kind of crazy message about the rules in OCS?"

"They should have axed all six of us. Still a shit deal, but I'd have felt better. Sometimes I think they did me a favor. Saved me ten months in the screwed up military."

"Yeah, I did the math too. So I kicked myself out of OCS."

Swede

For the moment, Swede was a corporal. Over a twelve-year career he had been up and down the enlisted ranks, working his way up to sergeant and in a single act getting busted down to private. Just before deployment to Vietnam he slugged a staff sergeant, whom Swede insisted had it coming. Now he was on the rise again, having worked his way back up to corporal. Swede gave no thought to regulations, and he worried even less about getting caught.

He was a huge guy with a shock of blonde hair. Two large front teeth came out when he smiled, the dental work of a rabbit mounted in the head of a water buffalo. He was a simple guy who laughed with his whole body and was quick with his fists. Swede spent his evenings drinking and playing poker. He told me the reason getting busted never bothered him was that he made more money at cards than he ever earned in military pay. I liked Swede but was careful never to make him mad, and never to play poker with him.

I was chatting with him outside his hooch when he came close and whispered, "Want to see something?" He led me

152

around the flak wall into his hooch. Sitting on his bunk was a young Vietnamese girl. She smiled up at me.

"I snuck her in three nights ago," Swede said. "She's my hooch girl. They can do it in Phan Rang. Why not me too?"

"How did you get her onto the firebase?"

"Easy. In a duffle bag."

"Who knows about this?"

"The guys on the gun, and now you. She stays in here during the day and the guys come in and visit, no funny business mind you. I wouldn't allow that. I'm not runnin' a whorehouse. Maybe if I needed the money, but I don't. The guys bring in food and stuff and play cards. She needs company 'sides my pretty face. She only goes out at night, and I make her wear a steel pot and a flak jacket so she kind of blends in."

"What about when she has to…"

"A helmet in the corner. Hey, I pay her five bucks a day."

Sure enough two nights later I saw a shadowy figure in a helmet and flak jacket, four and a half feet tall, floating among the guns, the shortest GI in military history. It went on for over a week. But things like this got out pretty fast. Once Top got wind of Swede's bunkmate he sent her out the main gate. Half a dozen soldiers stood on the berm and waved.

153

Forbidden Water

It was near the end of the dry season, when the air was the color of the ground. A fine brown powder dusted our skin and collected in mud specks in the corners of our eyes. It felt gritty between the teeth and smelled faintly of fish. Sweat ran in yellow tracks down our bodies. Rubbing produced a little black roll of dead skin and dirt.

> We wash with water from a well, which at this time of year yields something closer to wet sand than water. It is better than nothing I suppose. You have to get your own water with a bucket tied to a long rope. Our shower is a suspended 50 gallon oil drum with a punctured Coke can for a nozzle.

The water level in the well was six feet from the top. The

water came up brown and had all kinds of critters in it. Washing with it produced white patches of fungus on the skin, making some guys look like palominos. The medics told us it was tinea versicolor. We called it *the crud*. There was a better well 600 yards from our perimeter, just beyond the tree line. Even in the dry season it was full of clear water. It was too far from our perimeter to be safe, so Top declared the well off-limits.

The prohibition meant little to Swede. When no one was paying attention he would assemble his crew, hustle them into a truck loaded with empty ammo cans and head for the tree line. He always returned with a truckload of water you could see through, and that made him a hero for the day. As the monsoon season approached in June, bringing more rainfall, the approved well began to fill. But Swede still had it in his head that the forbidden well had the best water, and continued his forays out to the tree line.

It was just past noon when an explosion erupted at the tree line near the forbidden well. A plume of black smoke lifted above the treetops. We saw figures sprinting toward the battery. Swede was in the lead, pumping his arms and galloping in full stride. One of our guys grabbed his M16, hopped in a jeep and sped out the gate to meet them. Another climbed a guard tower and trained the machine gun in that direction. As the jeep rolled back through the main gate carrying the crew, Swede stood up and raised his arms in triumph. The small crowd gathered at the gate applauded. Swede bowed, almost toppling off the back of the jeep.

Our bulldozer went out later that day with a small detachment to drag the truck back. The crew found the hood fifty yards from the well. It was a 2½-ton truck, so it took a good size mine to blow the hood that far. The truck was completely destroyed and came back a pile of twisted debris. Somehow Swede and his three crewmen escaped with only minor burns and scratches. All Top said at formation was, "Now you know why that well is off-limits." Top knew when to let the lesson lay.

Swede made the story of his encounter with the mine more colorful with every telling. "After that mine blast I can't hardly hear now. But then again I couldn't hear so good before-hand either." Swede was probably telling the truth. He was old school artillery like Top, and had no use for earplugs. "But the mine was nothing," he loved to say. "It was the damn run back to the battery that just about killed me."

FO Fever

Storied infantry units bivouacked at Sherry, the Curahees of the 101st Airborne and the 50th mechanized infantry. I hung out with the forward observers because I loved the FO training at Ft. Sill and liked listening to stories from the field. After only a few weeks at Sherry I had forgotten that our FO team had just been chewed up at the battle of LZ Betty and wanted action.

This FDC job is sure boring. I am thinking seriously of becoming a forward observer. Sitting between four walls for 12 hours a day and getting very little exercise is getting to me. I'd rather be out and about. We've got a FO here now from the field. Think I'll talk to him in the morning. We have endless inspections, formations, "busy" projects, and everything else that goes with

*an Army without a war to fight.
I'd rather have the war - seriously.*

The drop in action did not last long. Fighting intensified
with the beginning of monsoon season. Thick cloud cover and
heavy rains reduced visibility at night to near zero and curtailed
air operations, making monsoon a good time of year for the
NVA and VC. They could pretty much waltz around at will.
Despite a sharp increase in fighting, I still lusted for action.

*Enemy activity has significantly
increased with the beginning of
July. This is their busy season
you know. A couple VC battalions have been roaming around
the area. We fired on one of
them just 1,000 meters off our
perimeter last Sunday morning.
Gunships also worked over the
area. That went on all morning.
Sunday morning is a favorite time
with the VC. The Sunday before
last I started my breakfast
three times. I'd get two bites
down when the siren would go
off for another fire mission.*

*Last week we were alerted for
a heli-borne operation. We were
told we would be going to Bu*

Prang, which is on the tip of the Parrot's Beak on the Cambodian border. But they have decided to send two guns from A Battery. I was looking forward to it; this place is so bloody boring.

I applied for FO school in early August. Every forward observer, even graduates of Ft. Sill, needed more training in Vietnam. After my first few minutes inside FDC and after listening to the FOs on the radio call in artillery with strange protocols and even stranger terminology, I understood. This was not something to be learned on the job. I was approved to attend FO school in October to replace a guy leaving the next month. My heart picked up a few beats at the thought of getting closer to the action.

Just before my departure Top pulled me aside. "The captain cancelled your FO school. He thinks you're too valuable because you have formal FDC training. And there'd be a shortage if you left."

I was crushed, thinking only of the endless tedium before me in this little firebase. "Top, what if I talked to him?"

"Won't do any good. He made up his mind. That's it."

I walked away mad, thinking, *thank you, Captain Crazy*.

Captain Crazy

His job was in the field, but his head was in the rear. Some guys would have said when it wasn't *up* his rear. He valued his reputation with the brass at battalion above all else. Appearance trumped the safety of his men, the operation of the battery and even our main mission to support the infantry. He followed the rules with priestly devotion, even when they made no sense or were downright dangerous.

His only friend was a female dog. He carried on long and intimate conversations with her seated on his lap. Walking by his hooch we could see them nose-to-nose, him gazing into her eyes and she hanging on his every word. He frequently took her into the latrine, which fired our imaginations for all manner of bestiality jokes. "She can't hold the toilet paper, but I bet I know what she's licking." When a battalion inspection loomed, he took her on practice runs in his jeep. He would lift his arm to points of interest and direct his comments to the passenger seat, soon to hold his colonel but now occupied by the dog. The junior officers called him Shaky. The enlisted men called him Captain Crazy.

By the time I got to Sherry the captain was already famous for an order that all the trucks and jeeps had to be parked facing out from their sandbag walls. The practice had been to face them into their protective barricades, so that the most damage an exploding mortar could do would be a couple blown tires. The captain wanted them facing outward because that was the protocol at his prior assignment—in Germany. He explained that facing them outward would make for a faster getaway. Where they would be getting away to, he did not say. Sure enough, the next mortar attack not only blew out front tires, but destroyed radiators and headlights. All this before they could make their getaways.

The captain insisted on adjusting our perimeter defensive targets himself. These were fixed targets that our sister batteries at Betty and Sandy used if we came under a ground attack, like the ones we used when Betty got overrun. The targets were set by calling in registration rounds. The captain brought the fire in so close that it blew up sections of barbed wire, tripped perimeter flares and sent shrapnel whistling through the compound. When Captain Crazy was setting defensive targets, everybody headed for cover. "If he tells me to bring that delta tango in one more meter," an FDC member said. "I'm just not going to do it. He can put me in jail if he wants."

The sky was royal blue that morning, the air light and alive. We were in the middle of a fire mission and shooting under a battery fire-for-effect command, all five howitzers firing as quickly as they could clear and reload. A radio call came into FDC from a chopper carrying the battalion commander. He was passing by when he saw the action and wanted to know what was going on. And his pilot needed to know where to fly so as not to cross paths with an artillery shell. I did not have time for a long conversation. I told him we were shooting for the 3/506 infantry, gave him a safe flight azimuth and signed off. The captain came running into FDC demanding to know who was in the chopper. When I told him he turned and went rushing out to the guns.

Swede came into FDC a few hours later and told us that the captain had run around to each gun, in the middle of the fire mission, ordering crewmen to put on their shirts.

"When the captain gets to my gun everybody looks up for a second. Shit, we were kinda busy you know, and we can't make out what he's saying till he gets up close and starts screamin' about fuckin' shirts. We're looking at him over our shoulders all twisted around because we're popping and clearing canisters."

Swede acted out the scene for us. Playing the captain, Swede put his fingers in his ears and held his elbows out like wings. "Boom...boom...boom," he said and rocked on his heels. He pulled one finger from his ear to free an arm, then waved it in the air shouting, "Shirt alert...shirt alert."

Swede continued the story, "Finally we get the gist of what he's trying to say and we look at him like he's some kind of fuckin' idiot, which he is. The howitzer goes off and he jumps out of his underwear, because he's got cherry ears and no earplugs. We go on about our business and he runs off in the direction of Gun 5. I never enjoyed ignoring an order so much in my entire life."

The road to our forward command post at Phan Thiet was mined. Supply helicopters were chronically short, forcing us to run convoys for basic supplies and sometimes ammo. This was not a leisurely motor through the countryside. It was a slow and painstaking job of sweeping the road for mines as we inched along and worried about VC attacks. The previous year three men from LZ Sherry had died from landmines. The guys who did this job wore flak jackets but never helmets. They had to bend over to use the sweeping equipment and sometimes probe into the ground. They did not want a helmet rolling off and detonating a mine. Wearing the helmet with a chinstrap brought its own dangers. Shrapnel striking the helmet could break a neck. Without the chinstrap the sweeper would have to hold the helmet with one hand and work the equipment with the other. The sweeping crews figured it was better to forget the helmet and use two hands. A lousy helmet wasn't going to save them from a mine blast in the face.

Captain Crazy said to the convoy team, "I want you looking sharp on this trip. Shirts, flak jackets, helmets. That goes for everybody."

The men who were sweeping for mines put up a fight. "Sir, we don't wear helmets when we sweep."

"I said *everybody*."

"They fall off, sir. They hit the ground and roll in front of you."

"I don't want the colonel flying over and seeing any of you out of uniform. There'll be an Article 15 for anybody I see not in uniform…and that includes helmets."

As the convoy snaked away from LZ Sherry toward Phan Thiet, I saw the men in front holding their helmets on their heads with one hand and fumbling with their sweeping equipment with the other. The captain stood wide-legged on the berm and watched through his binoculars until they were out of sight.

The Count

The fire missions that come over our radios sound like clips from a television serial. Infantrymen taking AK47 fire and mortars, or a chopper pilot adjusting artillery fire. Often it's hard to believe that it's all for real.

When a fire mission came in from the infantry we sounded the siren to bring the crews to their guns. A guy hopped on a map table to plot the target and compute the mission, while another figured up the same mission on the other map as a check. In under a minute we had a smoke round in the air. Often that was enough for the VC to break contact, knowing what was coming. On a good day the VC stayed to fight. Then we changed to HE rounds and went to *fire for effect*, all the guns firing as fast as their crews could clear and reload. *Fire for effect* always sent a quiver of excitement through me. I knew the coming roar would be all we had to give, and imagined the explosions when the shells landed in unison. I remembered being under a single exploding shell at Ft. Sill, but safe inside a bunker. What kind of hell was it out in the open under five of them? Sometimes the FO called for HE on the first round, when there was no time for smoke. That was never a good idea in our view, but the FO had the call. It meant his men were in desperate need. The FDC bunker was mighty quiet when that first shot went out.

After the action stopped the infantry policed the scene for bodies, but not like they were waltzing into an empty auditorium. There were booby traps, mines and hidden enemies to consider. Sometimes the VC broke contact in order to lure the infantry into position, so they could detonate mines or open up a second assault. When a reconnaissance helicopter worked the mission we got an early read on the body count, how many killed and wounded. Counts by chopper pilots were usually low because they only told us what the pilot could see out in the open. What mattered was what the infantry saw. Days later there could be reports from infantry patrols of mass graves containing eight, ten, sometimes fifteen bodies: all killed by artillery, dragged off and hurriedly buried.

We did a powerful lot of shooting these three nights. It was just like the good old days back in May and June. And you know, I was just as scared. From the traffic I could monitor over the radios, we killed well over 100 VC.

As soon as we knew a body count in FDC the number went out to the guns. While the veterans celebrated, the new guy usually turned inward. Now he was a killer. The faces of the dead and their families rose up in his imagination. He thought of their parents, wives, kids. He imagined what he had done to them. Some guys went quiet, some tried to figure a way out of the job. But everybody got over it, there was no choice. By the time I got my first body count, I had been shot at by snipers, had seen LZ Betty overrun and had experienced several mortar attacks. The way I looked at it, you either did the count, or you were the count.

No Such Thing As Routine

I was halfway to FDC during a routine mortar attack when a green flare went up. Gooks in the wire. A ground attack. The quad-50s must have lowered their fire into the concertina, because tracers ricocheted in crazy angles and the trip flares went off, casting a pink glow around the perimeter. I heard the new sound of claymores detonating, first off the southern perimeter and then all around. I figured the howitzers were leveling their tubes and loading beehive, shells with 6,000 little metal arrows that shredded everything in their path. I watched for a red flare.

As I ran, a fresh illumination round popped in the air and revealed something that chilled me more than enemy in the wire. A soldier behind a low bunker had his M16 leveled at someone running across the battery, about to take him down. I yelled. He turned and looked at me with wide, staring eyes. "That's a friendly," I said as I ran past him.

The red flare never came, and after it was over there were no bodies in the wire, or parts of bodies. They could have carried them off. Or it could have just been a probe to test us. Or maybe they were never there. The guard who popped the flare was a veteran, one of the best and good enough to convince me somebody had been out there. The soldier who drew a bead was a new guy. He had been through a couple mortar attacks, but at the thought of a ground attack he had lost his head. He would have been OK if he hadn't mixed up his greens and reds.

I could not feel superior. I remembered my own moment of paralyzing fear. I had been at Sherry a couple months and had been through enough action to consider myself a veteran. I was sleeping in my hooch when mortars started falling. There were only three or four. The howitzers were firing as I pulled on my gear and grabbed my M16. I was at the door about to leave for the FDC when I was seized by the thought that the explosions I heard were not howitzers but incoming mortar rounds. I knew better and forced myself out. I ran in a crouch past BIRTH CONTROLER, through the bang and the roar of its return fire. In a few strides I experienced a fear I did not know was possible. It tightened around my chest and made me helpless. I ducked behind a flak wall and crouched as low as I could get, convinced that if I stood up I would die. I crouched rigid and shaking until the firing stopped.

When I finally trotted into the FDC I heard, "Where've you been?"

"Trying not to get blown up," I said. I felt like a coward. At the same time I felt very much alive. Anybody who said he never panicked, not even once, was lying. At least that is how I came to live with the shame.

Later I again failed to appear in FDC during a mortar attack. I must have had a tough day filling sandbags. In the morning I woke up feeling great and popped into FDC bright as sunshine.

"Where were you last night?"

I said, "Sleeping, why?"

"Because we took incoming and when you didn't show we thought something might have happened to you."

"Well I'm fine. And thanks for coming to look for me."

Freddie

A computer the size of a baby rhino came on the scene, another piece of advanced technology from the Pentagon. It was a Field Artillery Digital Automated Computer, or Freddie FADAC, as we called it. In theory, Freddie would compute firing data more quickly and accurately than our manual slide rulers, protractors and charts. But it needed a lot of attention, beginning with its own dedicated generator. With the flip of the power toggle it wheezed as it turned itself on, and when fully awake it let out a low, steady groan. If a computer could be constipated that is how it would sound. The thing breathed out heat and made the FDC hooch even more oppressive. Freddie doubled our work. Everyday it needed to be fed weather data and friendly nighttime defensive positions, along with over 100 fixed defensive targets. For all the information in its circuitry, Freddie sometimes gave out crazy results. And it was slow, particularly when we had to run out to fire up the generator and then wait an eternity for all of its blinking lights and digital readouts to come to life. We came to calling it that "Fucking Freddie FADAC" and wanted to haul it to the trash dump.

Charlie stepped in. "For one thing we got orders to use it. Battalion's going to notice if it's in the trash dump. We at least have to turn it on during fire missions. Top comes in here during a mission, it better be on. As long as it's on, may as well try to make it work." So Charlie spent half his career feeding numbers into Freddie. He had help from Kim Martin, a quiet guy who acquired the name Metro Marty for his patience with putting in the mountain of meteorological numbers of wind, temperature and humidity for every fifty yards of elevation up to the moon. Sometimes there was help from volunteers, who sat at the keyboard and grumbled. When a fire mission came in Charlie was the one who started it up when everybody else was jumping on the map boards, and it was Charlie who ran out in the monsoon downpours to start its generator. Charlie discovered that Freddie was either close to the manual calculation, or way off. He suggested we shoot computer numbers when they were close, and ignore them when Freddie gave out wild data. Even so we never warmed to Charlie's friend and looked on it as piece of troublesome junk in our otherwise efficient FDC.

Junk Daddy

There were two Vietnams. Mine was the Vietnam of the field.

> This past week FDC has been a mad house. Most of the time we were talking to four people on two radios. Then we'd get two fire missions down at one time plus a report that our sister battery was taking mortar rounds. After coming off shift it took me at least an hour to relax enough to get to sleep. I don't have normal dreams anymore. All I dream about are machine guns and sandbags and helicopters.

The other was the Vietnam of the rear, a world of documents, forms, maintenance logs, reports, inspection summaries, protocols, manuals, regulations, organizational charts, manifests and inventory sheets. Its weapons were paper and ink. Its mission was to make things look like they were supposed to look. Reports went up the chain of command to senior officers who made more reports to even higher echelons. Careers hinged on paperwork, especially the dreaded Officer Efficiency Report. A comment on an OER or a checkmark in a single box could ruin a career.

The combat soldier was badly outnumbered by the hoards in the rear. For every soldier in the field there were six in rear echelon jobs. They populated supply, intelligence, personnel, medical, transportation, logistics, media relations, payroll and ordnance. The soldier in the field was helpless in the face of this vast and distant bureaucracy.

But LZ Sherry had a secret weapon—an aging supply sergeant. He was an elf of a man with a turned up nose out of a child's storybook. I met him on my second day at LZ Sherry.

"How long you been in country, sergeant?"

"Not long this time. I'm on my third tour."

"Third tour…in Vietnam?" I felt stupid before the words were out of my mouth.

"You know they made me stay state-side six months before I could come back this time." He took a drag on a cigarette. "To make sure I wasn't nuts I guess."

"You must be."

"Maybe. I like it here. Life is simple."

"You married?"

"Yeah, but like I said, life is simple here."

The supply sergeant moved between the two Vietnams with uncommon grace. He had friends up and down the length of Vietnam, from privates to generals, and across the Army, Navy, Air Force and Marines. He could travel anywhere he pleased and talk to anybody he wanted. Sometimes he disappeared for days. A guy could ask the sergeant for anything, and one day it would appear. We called him "Junk Daddy."

Generators were the standard of wealth in the field. Our small generators powered the mess hall refrigerator, the FDC and the radar tower. They also let a trickle of electricity through to a few lucky hooches, just enough to make a fan move—so slow you could count the blades.

One day an enormous Sky Crane helicopter hovered over the battery. These massive aircraft were used to move things like tanks and small buildings. We had never seen one at LZ Sherry. Swinging beneath it was a large diesel generator, the kind used in rear areas to cool barracks, power movie theaters and light officers' clubs.

Junk Daddy watched it descend. He said, "I been working on this one a long time."

"Where'd it come from?" I asked.

"Air Force."

"How'd you get it?"

"I know a guy."

"And…?"

"Don't ask."

"Come on, Junk, give me something here."

"Supply sergeant's a friend of mine."

"And…?"

"He wanted a few days at Puket."

"Nice place I hear."

"His colonel owed me a favor."

I looked at him and waited.

"Like I said, don't ask."

I have a picture of Junk Daddy on guard duty in one of the towers. He has a wool blanket pulled around his shoulders. It is before sunrise and cool in the eighties. In front of him sits a pack of Salem cigarettes, beside him is the landline handset off its cradle. He is in profile and looking east. The sky is violet at that time of the morning when the sun is still below the horizon, but its rays have found the clouds high in the sky, painting them pink and reflecting a warm glow onto his face. The face is tired from the night vigil, or perhaps wearied from years in combat—a portrait of a man with no home but Vietnam.

Cookie

Top came into FDC screaming and looking for me. His face was iridescent, his nose even brighter. "When a superior officer comes in here and gives you an order, you fucking do it. Do you understand?"

"He's the cook, Top. He doesn't run FDC," I said.

"I don't give a flying fuck. He's got an extra stripe. Do you goddamn fucking understand?"

I gave him the look.

"Don't just stand there like some idiot. You got a mouth. Out of it I want to hear you understand."

"Yes, First Sergeant."

He turned and walked out. The other men in FDC did not say a word; they just looked at me. The new guys had just gotten their first taste of the first sergeant in action. I expected his tantrums by this time, but hated being humiliated in front of the crew.

The incident began when the sergeant in charge of the mess hall, Cookie, came into FDC with a routine supply requisition. I was on the radio when he put the paper in front of me and said, "Send this in, right now." He was in the habit of bullying the people who worked for him and pushing people around when he could. People put up with him because he was a terrific cook. He could turn little tin cans of C Rations into a feast. In the Army a good cook could get away with homicide if his beef stew reminded the troops of mom.

"Sergeant, I'm busy," I told him. "I'll get to it when I can." I did not try to hide my irritation.

"No, you'll do it now."

"No, I'll do it when I can. I got something I have to do now."

Cookie grabbed the paper and stomped out. He must have run straight to Top because it was not long before Top stormed into FDC. After Top finished with me, Cookie came back. Without a word he put the piece of paper in front of the radio and left. After that I never saw him inside FDC again. I suspect Top gave him the same treatment he gave me. I put the requisition through the next day when I was good and ready.

Mad Minute

For one minute every month, at the stroke of midnight, we fired off every weapon in the battery. It was an orgy of firepower pouring out of everything in the battery with a muzzle, a kind of military masturbation. The minutes before midnight were quiet. Crews of men stood ready at their weapons—magazines and breaches loaded. Soldiers lined the berm with rifles, grenade launchers and pistols tensed in their hands. The men and machine guns in the towers were single, still silhouettes. At midnight a howitzer angled high into the sky fired, but all else remained quiet. Seconds later, with the gentle pop of an illumination round, the battery erupted. Four howitzers fired as one. The quad-50s spat white fire and before long the tips of their barrels glowed red against the black night. The Duster cannons put out low hanging airbursts just over the berm, like a string of Christmas lights. From the guard towers tracers glided out in long red arches and died in the darkness. The small weapons from the berm sounded like popcorn against the heavy background of howitzers and quad-50s. A second illumination round lit the sky, bringing a sudden quiet, with a lonely rifle burst trailing behind. Clouds of smoke drifted through the silence. In this post orgasmic moment we imagined that we had just showed the enemy, by nature voyeurs, that ours was bigger than theirs.

Besides its entertainment value, the mad minute was a monthly maintenance check, guaranteeing that all weapons were in working order. Just as important, it served to educate new guys on the sounds of friendly weapons in the confusion of battle. During a real attack it was important to know if an explosion was a VC mortar landing or one of our howitzers—to tell the difference between an M16 and an AK47—to know if a funny sound was a mortar leaving its tube and headed this way, or a Thumper firing at the enemy, or maybe the guy in the next bunk with a bad stomach. When things got hot a soldier's ears were his best friends.

One morning after a mad minute, a Duster crewmember came into the FDC bunker. "I want to put in for a Purple Heart." The Duster crews were attached to our battery but not in our chain of command, so they did not appear at formation or help with the maintenance of the firebase. You could pick them out by their long hair and general scruffy appearance, something Top would never have tolerated. He called them "fucking parasites." This one had not shaved for a week and looked pregnant. He pointed to a bandage taped to his stomach, "I got hit last night."

"What happened?" I asked.

"Shrapnel," he scratched beside the bandage.

"There was no hostile fire last night."

"One of my rounds caught the top of the berm and the shrapnel got me in the stomach."

How could it miss? I thought. I said, "So you shot yourself."

"Yeah I guess so, if you put it that way."

"What other way is there to put it?"

"Hey man, this was live fire and we're in a combat zone."

"True. And?"

"And I got treated by a medic and all. You can ask Doc."

"How come I didn't hear about the Medevac chopper?"

"Didn't need it, but hey I still got shot. You get hurt in a combat zone, especially shot like me, you get the purple, right?"

"I have to tell you, they're for guys who get messed up by the VC or the NVA or maybe even a kid throwing a stick, but it's got to be the enemy. You can't give yourself a Purple Heart."

"How do you know?"

"I'm pretty sure about this one."

"All I want you to do is put it on a form somewhere, you know, and send it in."

"I don't think I can do that, but I tell you what. You get Top to OK it, and I'll do the paperwork." At this he brightened and went looking for the first sergeant.

I could not see Top's hooch from the FDC bunker, but I kept a watch in that direction. It was only minutes until my man came back into view. There was a dark look on his face, and as he passed by, the wounded warrior turned and raised a middle finger in my direction.

Smoke

We called him Smoke. He was the staff sergeant in charge of the gun crews, riding hard on five platoons of teenage gun bunnies. His skin was ebony black, which helped to show off a dazzling display of teeth. On one front tooth was an inlaid gold star, on the other a red heart. When Smoke smiled it was the Fourth of July.

"When I was in Korea in the early days," he said, "the Chinese mounted these human wave attacks. That's when we brought the .50-cals over. I don't think we was supposed to because the fifties was supposed to be anti-aircraft, not anti-personnel. The Geneva Convention, or some shit like that. Well, we did it anyway. Had to. When they come at us we just chop 'em down. The bodies pile up but they kept comin', climbed right over 'em. We'd end up firing just about straight up they was piled so high." He flashed a pyrotechnic smile, "The wave attacks didn't last long."

181

The Secretary

Secretary of the Army Stanley Resor came to visit in early July. It took a week to get ready. Captain Crazy, for all his odd behavior, was brilliant in hosting dignitaries. He understood the perverse logic that in order to look like a combat unit to his superiors, we had to *not* look like a combat unit.

The first job was to cut the grass growing on the berm and sprouting between hooches. It had grown wild and tall with the monsoon rains. I was assigned the berm behind my hooch. We had no equipment for cutting grass, so the captain told us to use shovels. I swung the shovel and filled the air with flying grass. I looked over to the quad-50 bunker and saw guys cutting the grass on the roof, where it grew taller than on the ground. When they were finished it looked like a bad haircut.

The seats on our jeeps were torn and filthy, so the captain ordered them reupholstered—with sandbags. He wanted signs put up, with red backgrounds and yellow lettering. We made one that said LATRINE. Another went on the hooch that Top and Smoke shared that read TOP AND SMOKES' HOOCH. The captain did not notice the punctuation mistake, or we sure-ly would have done it over. There were signs on the low ammo bunkers beside each howitzer that read *Low Ceiling*.

Two days before the visit an advance team of specialists arrived. Their job was to map out the secretary's route around the compound, make a rough schedule, take pictures and cover the event for the newspapers. During the day they chatted with the quad-50 crews and walked around the howitzers with their hands on their hips. At night they stayed in their hooches. They knew a mortar attack was always likely. With the guns firing H&I and illumination all night, they would as likely think the bang a mortar as a howitzer. In the dark they could not have found their way around anyway. So at night the advance team stayed inside, like rabbits in a warren.

With the daylight one of the advance team came into the FDC bunker in his perfect uniform and entertained us with war stories, not his own but ones he had collected on his travels. It was obvious he had never touched an M16 in Vietnam. Leino said to him, "Sir, did they brief you on our new radar? It's classified, experimental and top secret, so we can only show it to people who've been briefed."

"Of course."

"If you want to see it, I'll take you over."

"Yeah, I've got a few minutes, I'd like to see it in operation."

Half an hour later Leino came back alone. "He's still there staring at the screen. The radar guys are feeding him all kinds of bullshit about radar that bends and sees around corners. He started to take notes and they wouldn't let him. I left when they started on rays that can penetrate buildings."

The arrival of the Secretary of the Army came with all the expected drama. Half a dozen Cobra gunships thundered over the horizon. In their midst were two Hueys. The Hueys landed but the Cobras stayed in the air. Secretary Resor walked through the main gate surrounded by a small army of colonels, our captain close by his side. We were ready in FDC to show him the nerve center of the battery, but he never showed. His visit lasted less than ten minutes, barely enough time to see the new latrine sign.

By military standards Captain Crazy must have earned an A+ on the visit. Secretary Resor played his role. He came, he saw, he left.

God's Shower Room

July brought the monsoon season in earnest to the Central Highlands. Most evenings at four o'clock sharp, thick clouds rolled down from the mountains and brought with them torrential rains. Walls of water turned the ground to soup, and when the sun set a dark descended so profound that a hand held out disappeared, dissolved by the night. The veterans went about with their eyes open but blind, navigating by the picture in their heads. New guys relied on flashlights, good for only a few feet in the downpour. With the rising sun the clouds moved back to the mountains, leaving the daylight hours clear and sunny. The clouds looked down, purple and sullen from their mountaintops, waiting patiently for the evening.

The countryside erupted in lush, violent greenery, while the warm daytime air sucked up moisture and made our valley into a great, sweltering sauna. The well filled high with clear water. Puddles the size of small lakes filled the compound. Guys floated in them on air mattresses and wrestled shin deep in the water. Everywhere wet clothing dried on the concertina wire, looking like a great outdoor laundry. A new trash pit filled to the top with muddy water. It became a swimming pool, and a jeep backed to the edge became a diving platform. I snapped a picture of a boy in mid backflip, suspended above the distant mountain peaks.

With the setting sun the clouds rolled down from the mountains and visited another deluge upon us. I saw Top through the twilight one evening strolling naked in the rain, his medicine ball stomach leading the way. A bar of soap hung on a rope around his neck. He was singing. This looked like a great way to take a shower, so early the next evening I stepped into the rain and lathered up. The water felt colder than I expected and soon I was shivering. But now covered with soap, I was committed. I stood naked in the frigid downpour using my hands to help the soap off my body. Guys walking by in jackets and ponchos looked at me. Back in my hooch I wrapped up in my wool blanket until I stopped shaking. The next morning I got up with a cold that lasted two weeks.

Taste of Luxury

I got my first pass to the rear in late September after five months in the field. I wrote to Kathleen from Phan Rang airbase.

The place is enormous. It has a complete bus network to get people around. First thing, I took a shower with clean water and out of real pipes. It made me feel five pounds lighter. I took about four showers a day and loved every one of them.

The airbase has an air conditioned theater with soft seats, popcorn, flush toilets, the whole bit. It's like a trip back to the states. I took in a couple floor shows at the NCO club.

The outdoor cocktail lounge is lined with palm trees and over-looks the airbase from its perch halfway up the mountain. Mixed drinks are - would you believe it - 15 cents. And the airmen here get combat pay!

The Major's Night Out

Platoons of clerks at battalion kept track of ammunition. Every morning they wanted to know how much we had fired and how much we had on hand. But they did more than write the numbers down and tally up the figures. They tried to control how much ammo we shot. They had a sharper eye on LZ Sherry because we shot so many fire missions and every month ate up a mountain of ammo, more than any battery in central Vietnam they were always telling us. They never complained about fire missions, but took out after the defensive firing we did at night. "Why did you shoot so much H&I last night? You need to build up your HE reserves for fire missions. Could you start H&I later or maybe end it earlier in the morning? See if you can cut back on illumination this month."

To keep everyone happy we began a program of creative reporting. We inflated the number of rounds we shot on fire missions and mortar attacks, and under-reported what we shot at night for H&I and illumination. This gave us a secret stash to maintain as much defensive firing at night as we needed. One of the important things I did in FDC was to make sure the numbers looked credible to the rear. I tried to give numbers that kept the clerks a little unhappy, otherwise they would have gotten suspicious. Few people outside of FDC knew about the scheme. Top and the battery commander knew, but pretended not to. It was one of the silent deals that made a firebase work. After reading *The Godfather* on nightshift, I thought of myself as LZ Sherry's consigliere, a Tom Hagen in fatigues.

No officer over the rank of captain could spend the night in the field, that was the rule. We had a lot of brass out to visit Sherry, even a one-star general. They differed in the intelligence of their questions and the stupidity of their recommendations, but they had one thing in common—they all left before sunset.

We were stunned when we learned that a major from Phan Rang would be spending the night at LZ Sherry. Even more suprising, he was in charge of ammunition supply and the guy who gave us all the grief about nighttime perimeter defense. He came into FDC taking short, dainty steps. His body was round and well scrubbed. In civilian life he could have been the wine critic for a food magazine. He tried to make us like him. "I needed to get out of Phan Rang for a few days, and I've heard so many good things about your firebase here, I thought I'd come out for a little visit. I'm staying with your captain, and I think I'll trot on over to his quarters and say hello. I'd like to come back later tonight, if you don't mind me being a bird on the shelf. Just so we don't get a mortar attack tonight," he said with a little laugh. We smiled to be polite.

There was no night as terrible as the first night in the field. On a cloudy night the black was so thick you could almost grab handfuls of it. Small noises materialized into a menagerie of creatures, all of them hostile. The night had barely laid its heavy hand upon the battery when the major appeared inside

FDC. Under his helmet his face was whiter than I remembered. "It's dark out there," he said.

"Yes, sir," the three of us on duty all said at once.

"Think we'll get hit tonight?"

I spoke for the group. "Maybe, sir."

"What was that?" He snapped his head around.

"Just a radio squawk, sir."

A howitzer fired and the major's head whirled in the other direction. "My God, is that a mortar attack?"

"No, sir. Just H&I. We shoot those every so often to keep VC off the perimeter."

"God. I know Sandy got hit two nights ago."

"Yes, sir."

"Think they're still around?"

"Maybe, sir."

A howitzer fired again and in a little time an illumination round popped. The major poked his head out the door and around the flak wall to have a look, keeping his body behind. When his head returned he said, "Those things really light things up."

"Yes, sir. They do."

Just then our radar unit called in movement 200 yards to the southwest, near the streambed where the VC mortar crews typically set up. The radio operator called out the coordinates, another guy jumped to the map board and within half a minute we had firing instructions to BAD NEWS for three rounds, airburst. The gun was immediately beside the FDC bunker and when it fired the major ducked his head at each shot.

"Is that the Cong?" Now he was in full battle mode. "Maybe we should shoot another round."

"Probably just a water buffalo, sir. That's what it usually

191

is. There's no more movement, but radar's got an eye on it."

"Good, should we shoot illumination so they can check?"

"Radar doesn't need it, sir. And we just shot illumination a few minutes ago."

The major stayed in FDC most of the night pacing and flinching and fighting imaginary VC. In the morning he left on a chopper for Phan Rang, cutting short his vacation. Before leaving he said, "I know my guys press you about ammunition, but after last night I don't think you people shoot enough. I will never again question your H&I."

The major was true to his word for two entire days, when the second-guessing and empty headed suggestions took up again. One night in the field did not change a rear echelon desk jockey. But now he had felt the dread that grips even hardened veterans in the field, and still he worked to take away our night-time ammo. For this act of betrayal we gave him a field promotion to REMF—rear echelon motherfucker.

He was the only officer above captain who ever spent the night at LZ Sherry. Some regulations were too important to ignore.

POW

He was a child committing an act of war. We nabbed him
in our concertina wire putting rubber bands around the trip
flares. The VC and NVA often sent children to disable the flares
before a ground attack. This made it easier for sappers to penetrate and blow holes in the wire, leading the way for NVA and
VC regulars to come pouring through. We were already on edge
from a special alert that had come down a few days before, and
we were taking more than the usual amount of mortar fire. Days
earlier a crew servicing the trip flares in the outer wire had discovered an anti-personnel mine. It was a homemade device:
explosive material and four batteries in a plastic bag, with two
bamboo sticks and wires for a detonator. It did not matter to a
lot of guys that the enemy disabling our flares was a kid.

The soldier who caught the boy hauled him into the compound at rifle point. He looked to be around eight years old, just
a whisper of a boy. His shoulder joints stuck up from his body
in two knobs. He was dressed in a pair of shorts and Ho Chi
Minh sandals, made with tire treads and strips of inner tube.
He was crying. A crowd gathered and soon a heated discussion

boiled up.

"He's just a little kid, let him go."

"Bullshit, these kids are soldiers. He's a fuckin' prisoner as far as I'm concerned."

"He's faking those tears, they train 'em to do that, and I'll bet he's a lot older than he looks."

"They don't train these kids. They threaten their families or they pay them to do this shit."

"He did this in broad daylight, right in front of us. He's too stupid to be a soldier."

"He's a soldier if he's working for the gooks."

Voices rose to shouting. The boy knew no English, and we could manage only a few words of Vietnamese, none of them useful. We must have seemed like white giants to him, some with yellow hair that many Vietnamese had never seen and loved to touch when given the chance. The prisoner stood surrounded by these strangely colored behemoths as they bellowed at each other in their flat, guttural language.

In came Top. He was never very far from the action. He listened without saying a word. With no explanation Top pulled his .45 and said, "I'm gonna shoot the little fucker right here and now." He leveled the pistol at the boy's chest.

The crowd fell silent. The boy stopped crying. There was a moment of stillness when the unthinkable was about to occur.

"NO," we shouted together. One soldier stepped between Top and the boy. Then all was chaos and shouting again.

Top put away his pistol. "OK, girls, but get that little shit out of my battery." He walked away disgusted.

The boy stared with wide, unseeing eyes. His entire body began to shake. The soldiers who wanted him in a POW camp now petted his shoulder, rubbed his arms, crouched to look into his eyes and said soothing words to him. The kid started to cry again. Someone brought out a Hershey bar, maybe the greatest weapon of goodwill ever deployed by the U.S. military. The boy stopped crying and looked around. He took the candy bar and gave a smile that would melt the paint off a howitzer. That was all the encouragement we needed. Guys scurried off in search of more stuff. They piled the boy high with cartons of cigarettes, candy, C rations and a magazine or two. He staggered out the main gate hardly able to carry it all, but carrying a message from Top that needed no translation.

Words for Posterity

Two boys started wailing on each other in the center of the battery. They were crewmen on different guns, and the argument had been festering for weeks. Now their scrawny arms flew at one another. A crowd was forming.

I was in the mess hall and Top was at the next table. Top exploded from his chair and charged out the door, me right behind him. He marched with long, determined strides. His face was already scarlet, which meant trouble for anyone in its kill zone. He parted the spectators with a single breaststroke. He grabbed each combatant by an arm—like chicken wings in his meaty fists—and pulled the kids apart. Top then uttered the most memorable line in the history of the Vietnam conflict. He said, "Don't you boys know that violence never solves anything?"

The Vietnamese Within

Five Vietnamese worked in the mess hall and lived in hooches in a corner of the firebase. They had to live in the compound because Top would not let Vietnamese civilians travel in and out of the firebase. He was not concerned about what might be carried in, so much as the information that might walk out, such as guard duty routines, habits of work crews, defensive installations and the layout of the firebase.

Mama-san ruled over the two boys and two girls. When mad she let loose a sing-song invective that cut like a dull saw. Of the two girls, we judged Cindy to be the cute one. She had breasts that were barely there, only a hint of hip and a sideways rock in her walk. Still she inflamed erotic imaginations across the battery, a ninety pound sex symbol with a funny walk and a shy smile. She knew almost no English, or pretended not to. Cindy kept to herself and just smiled at the teasing from the boys. That did not stop them from bragging. "She invited me into her hooch last night. I swear." It was all make-believe. Mama-san kept a close eye on her girls. When she saw any kind of special attention going to Cindy, she moved in and scolded everyone away.

Mama-san wanted the attention for herself. She loved to be teased. Comments about her great beauty brought a toothy grin. When asked about her many lovers, she gave a girlish turn of the head. She could not get enough of it. But no one ever bragged about being invited into Mama-san's hooch.

The two boys, Slick and Wan, were in their mid-teens. They unloaded supplies into the mess hall, cleaned the dining area and fetched water. An ancient 16mm movie projector found its way onto the firebase. Slick and Wan loved the Westerns and would bounce up and down firing mock six-shooters with their fingers. They learned to play basketball and one day Slick beat three guys in a game of HORSE. Wan learned to throw a football further than half the guys in the battery. Every week their English got a little better.

It was Top's idea to start a school fund for the boys. There was no mention of Cindy, or the other girl who appeared to be past school age. The boys came from poor families and had no hope of ever getting an education. What little they earned went home to their parents. Top asked everyone to pitch in a dollar a month for six months. It would be enough to send both boys to school for three years, where they would have a place to stay and a private tutor. If they earned good grades they would get their first two years of college free. They would soon be eligible for the Vietnamese draft, and going to school would delay their military service.

A barber came to the firebase every week, the one exception to Top's residency rule. We could dress as we wanted below the neck, but our heads belonged to Top and he wanted them regulation at all times. It was easy to throw on shirts and hats and long pants when dignitaries dropped in, but the hair always had to be ready for show time. The barber came through the gate and went straight to his station, a chair located in the shade of a hooch close to the latrine. He cut hair with a cigarette hanging from his mouth, did not talk much, and spent more time looking around the compound than attending to the head in front of him. He was not allowed to walk around the firebase. Memories of the previous barber who had led a ground attack, and ended with only his upper body dangling in the wire, still resonated. In the afternoon he went out the gate richer, but knowing no more about the firebase.

The only civilians we let close to our perimeter were a middle aged man and two girls. They sold bracelets, Playboy bunny pins and all sorts of trinkets out of an open briefcase. We gave them a little sun shelter of ammo boxes and a culvert half. I bought a headband from them that had stitched on it VIET<WAR>NAM—like I needed a reminder.

I often wonder what became of Mama-san, Cindy, Slick and Wan. Were they among the 100,000 civilians who died fleeing the advancing NVA, or the 170,000 who died in re-education camps, or the 150,000 who perished in forced labor camps? Did the NVA declare them collaborators, and like 200,000 others simply execute them?

Casualty statistics are from: R.J. Rommel, *Vietnamese Democide: Estimates, Sources, and Calculations*, 1997; *Osprey Warrior 135, The North Vietnamese Army Soldier*, 1958-75.

Friendly Farmers

Every civilian was a potential enemy. A few weeks before my arrival at LZ Sherry two Vietnamese kids managed to roll a fifty-five gallon drum of CS military-grade tear gas up to the gate and blow it. From basic training I knew it stung the skin even through clothing, and made the eyes water to near blindness. Enough of it caused vomiting. A large cloud floating through the firebase would have been a fine beginning to a ground attack. Nobody ever explained how the two guys rolling the barrel ever got that close.

We kept a special eye on the people off our perimeter working the rice paddies and tending cattle. We worried they could be planting mines, hiding weapons, picking up information about the battery or waiting to take a pot shot. This was not an imagined danger. At our sister battery to the north at firebase Sandy, a soldier in a guard tower watched a farmer move his grazing cattle toward the perimeter. He noticed a line of six VC with rifles moving single file behind the cattle. They were about 400 yard out when the quad-50s opened up and resolved the situation. Whenever we got uncomfortable with farmers and their cattle getting too close to our wire, we put a spray of M16 fire over their heads to shoo them away.

One afternoon I hitched a ride to the rear on a Chinook, the big double-bladed supply helicopter. We were about 100 feet in the air and riding with the cargo bay open. A bullet came zinging up through the opening and rattled around the fuselage. A friendly farmer had gotten off a lucky shot, probably with an old carbine used against the French. Anything newer would have done more than bounce around. Some of us wanted to turn back and go after the guy. The Air Force crewman laughed and said, "Happens all the time."

A directive came down that said we could not shoot at someone unless he shot at us first. When Top read the piece of paper at formation he could barely get the words out. Not long after this we spotted kids poking around the trash dump. Instead of sending a few rounds over their heads, a soldier took out after them on foot. He chased one kid all over a rice paddy. When he caught the boy he found that he was only stealing spoiled butter.

A few weeks later we watched more kids playing off the perimeter where our bulldozer was clearing brush. The prior month near LZ Betty two Duster tracked vehicles had been blown up by landmines in separate incidents. The next morning when our bulldozer went out to resume work, the operator discovered a Chicom anti-tank mine, command detonated. He said there was a group of civilians gathered around it that dispersed when he approached. That afternoon we asked for permission to take action against personnel within 300 yards of the perimeter, a request that was denied.

The rules of engagement changed by the day and talk of the events at LZ Betty grew loud around the firebase, about rifles being locked away and guards not being allowed to shoot. Would we be next? The talk was angry and exaggerated. It reflected our frustration during the drawdown of U.S. troops, when policies were designed to show America's declining involvement in the conflict. But we knew conditions were as dangerous as ever, perhaps more precarious for LZ Sherry because of dwindling infantry support.

It was Sunday morning. I was on the berm with First Lieutenant Rudewieck, executive officer and second in command. The XO was a West Point graduate and looked it. He was on a second tour in Vietnam, had little use for regulations and was incurably trigger-happy. I loved being around him because he was always looking for action. When he could not find any he manufactured it. He held binoculars to his eyes. Without lowering them he said, "Gaydos, get back to FDC, we're gonna waste some gooks." I looked in that direction and even without binoculars I could see a line of VC walking along the tree line in plain view, as if to taunt us. I sprinted to FDC. The XO was already on the line at one of the guns with the azimuth and distance. The guy had a compass and map in his head. I called up all five guns and had them ready ten HE rounds. I gave each gun separate aiming data to create a train of explosions along the tree line. I did not sound the siren because that would alert the VC. When I gave the "fire" command, the guns roared in unison and poured out fifty shells in a little over a minute. Inside FDC we felt the pounding. The XO added fifty yards and ordered a repeat. A crewman later told me 200 yards of green tree line disappeared behind a wall of black smoke. The XO was not satisfied. He told me to call in gunships. In ten minutes a Cobra gunship was working over the area. It was fearsome to behold. Rockets screamed from its haunches and made bright explosions behind the tree line. Red tracers rained from the machine gun in its nose.

The line of VC we had seen was the corner of two VC battalions. More gunships rotated to the spot and we poured out artillery fire all morning. When the shooting was over Captain Crazy came into FDC. Ever mindful of the directives about engaging the enemy he said, "The XO told me you were on the berm with him when you took sniper fire."

I said, "Yes, sir. Just missed us. We're lucky to be alive."

The Little People

Orders from the Pentagon: we could no longer call the enemy *gooks*. We could only say VC or NVA. We could no longer use nicknames for civilians and ARVN forces, no matter how benign.

Captain Crazy was in FDC while we were plotting nightly defensive positions when…

One of my men used the term "little people" over the radio – which is a radio nickname for the Vietnamese regulars. Well I thought the battery commander would faint. That's the type of thing our officers get excited about. The other night while we were being mortared, a "little people" outpost got overrun, and the next morning a U.S. Cavalry company got overrun by an

NVA battalion near here. Still we must be polite in what we call our friends and our beloved enemy. I would really prefer to respect my superiors. They insist upon making that impossible.

Soon word came down to use ARVN artillery in support when we had the chance. It was part of the Vietnamization of the war effort. An opportunity came up when we got a call from the infantry to soften up a suspected VC location. There was no firefight, no urgency to the mission. We called it into the ARVN artillery battery in our sector. We told the infantry forward observer and he said, "Oh God."

The marking smoke round took forever. When it came the FO said, "I really don't know how to adjust off that. It could be RIGHT 800, ADD 1500, but who knows? Give them the coordinates again and tell them to start over. In the meantime we're taking cover."

The second smoke round was a repeat of the first. The FO said, "How about we cancel this mission. Unless you Einsteins think we should fire for effect."

We cancelled the mission and concluded that even though the Vietnamization of the fighting was not going well, our radio protocol was impeccable.

Full Court

Everybody needed a way to cope. Some guys turned to booze or drugs. Others bought the company of women. All these involved putting something into one's body, or into someone else's. I played basketball.

The court was a small patch of concrete with a plywood backboard and a naked hoop. We played in combat boots and cut off fatigue pants. The rough concrete wore the treads on our boots down to nothing and sanded the ball smooth. The slab was only big enough for half-court games, which turned into bludgeoning matches. We milled about under the basket shoving and flailing. Rank, age and size counted for nothing. We called our own fouls, but only pussies called fouls. We played every day. During monsoon season we splashed around the court, trying to hold onto a wet, slippery ball. In the dry season, dust everywhere, the sweat ran brown down our bodies.

I had the white man's disease, I could not jump. My leap was little better than standing on my toes. I compensated by not being able to dribble or shoot. But I understood the game. I knew where to be for rebounds, and how to get free for an easy gi'me shot. I worked on passing, which made me popular with the ball hogs. My greatest ability had little to do with basketball, I could run all day, and my greatest value to the team was my willingness to sacrifice my body to the cause.

At Ft. Sill, after giving blood, I was supposed to take it easy for a couple days. But my battalion team was in the post tournament and I believed it could not win without me. Midway in the third quarter I felt my heart pounding like I had never felt before. I could not breath and my chest felt like someone was sitting on me. The world turned to flickering dots and on my way down to the floor I thought, *I'm finally getting out of the Army...in a casket.* The doc at the hospital said, "There's nothing wrong with you. Just take it easy for a few days." When I told this to my sergeant, the one who hated Catholic basketball players, he said, "Bullshit." That day I was back on duty, and the next day back on the court. I was crazy for the game.

Junk Daddy came up with some stray bags of concrete and work began on expanding the court. It was my first experience of laying concrete, and it convinced me to stay away from this line of work after the Army. The new court stretched forty feet and had a basket at each end. We were now ready for full court games. Real basketball.

I remember the first game, not the final score or who played, but the sound of ten sets of combat boots thundering down the length of new concrete, like kettledrums at the opening of a symphony. Full court opened up the action for fast breaks, give-and-go, high screens and backdoor passes. Every game brought a new mix of players, and now there were spectators. A kid who never got picked in school sank a half court shot and bowed to the crowd. A jock put on a show with a pirouette and a kiss of the ball off the backboard, earning a little applause. A bad pass to the groin brought groans from the stands.

What I lacked in talent I made up for in stamina. I could run, and from childhood the heat never bothered me. After a twelve hour shift inside the FDC cave, I loved running the court with the thermometer at triple digits. The highlight of my day was sprinting past the high school star bent over with his hands on his knees and sucking air. Full court basketball kept me sane.

Seven in a Jeep

"It's not fair," began the typical rant. "We're in sandbag hooches, to where you can hardly breath at night, and the guys in the rear are getting out of bed to adjust the air conditioning. The water's brown we wash in, you shouldn't have to wash in colored water. We dance under mortars every couple a' nights out here, and they're at the movies deciding if they want popcorn. All night, two feet from a snoring ape, a lot different from the hooch girls who do their laundry, polish their boots and God knows what else. That's what really rubs raw. Swede gave it a try and got away with it for a while. Good goddamn for him."

It seemed our fortunes had taken a lucky turn when a band of prostitutes out of Phan Thiet showed up. They had walked the entire distance. They erected a tent, which drew an instant crowd of soldiers, some sprinting out of the compound and others taking jeeps and trucks. Captain Crazy looked out to see half his battery clustered around the tent, like sperm competing for a single canvas egg. He rushed out of his hooch to take command of the situation, only to discover he had nothing to ride. So he took out running. When the troops saw him coming they scattered in all directions. Jeeps and trucks piled high with bodies sped off, leaving clouds of brown dust. Soldiers on foot scattered left and right along the perimeter. At the tent the captain stood alone with the prostitutes, jerking his head from north to south, east to west, looking for stragglers. He turned to the prostitutes and started waving his arms. Within half an hour the tent was gone. Over the next hour the men and vehicles leaked back into the battery, all with a studied air of innocence.

That night the captain claimed to have identified the men in one of the jeeps. His problem was what to do with them. They had broken no regulation, disobeyed no order, damaged no equipment, brought no aid or comfort to the enemy. The captain went looking for a reason to discipline the men and make an example of them. He found it buried in the operator's manual for the jeep, in Item (4) of Paragraph c in Section I of Chapter 2: loading beyond the capacity of a vehicle meant for four personnel. In one of his last official acts, the captain gave each of the perpetrators an Article 15 for riding seven in a jeep.

Boom-Boom Girls

The next week a new battery commander arrived, and a week after that the girls returned. Now there were rules. The girls could come only on Wednesdays, had to remain outside the wire, and were to be gone by nightfall. Soldiers had to have condoms with them as required equipment. Top's fingerprints were all over the new arrangement.

Business was conducted under metal culvert halves used for lining ditches, raised on walls of artillery ammo boxes. Two structures sat side by side, sharing a common wall, and each sheltering a fold-up cot. Army blankets covered the openings at each end. A mama-san ran the business from the shady side of the ammo boxes. She sat on a tubular metal chair with a red vinyl seat, the kind made for cafeterias. It had come almost completely apart and leaned so far to the side it was a wonder it stayed upright. Mama-san collected the money, controlled the queue and kept the peace. When a new customer came into view she flashed a smile of dazzling white teeth and made the universal gesture of rubbing her middle finger over the top of her index finger. "Boom-boom five dolla," she said. When not recruiting business she mooched Salem cigarettes from waiting GIs.

It was a tidy operation. Customers lined up at one end, went in the front blanket and out the back. Three girls worked in quick rotation, while the five-dollar notes accumulated in Mama-san's pocket. A soldier said to me on a Thursday morning at breakfast, "Yesterday I just didn't have it. And you know Mama-san doesn't give you all day." He paused. "But she gave me a rain check."

Captain Joe

My first impression of the new battery commander was of another lifer who would be more trouble than he was worth.

Well, we got a new BC last week, another West Point Graduate. He ain't worth a damn either as far as I'm concerned. I'm afraid I just can't see the utility of spit 'n' polish and military protocol in Vietnam.

Never was a first judgment so wrong. Captain Joe immediately tolerated the boom-boom girls, a minor risk for a career officer. In a single act he raised the morale of the entire battery, even of the guys who were not paying customers. Some went out just to horse around and maybe keep track of the guys who were there for business. The area turned into a kind of enlisted man's club for a few hours every Wednesday.

The minesweepers immediately went back to their preferred practice of using both hands to operate the equipment. With the troop drawdown we ended up as the only artillery battalion left in the field in all of Central Vietnam. With only sporadic infantry and chopper support it grew mighty lonely. As a result we ran more convoys to Phan Thiet for basic supplies. It was a relief not to have to worry about the battalion colonel flying over and seeing the sweepers out of uniform.

Captain Joe went on to prove himself a steady battery commander, able to act in the interests of his troops, while keeping the rear echelon clerks and colonels at bay. On occasion I found myself alone with him, and it was at these conversations that I discovered what a smart and decent man he was. One evening I said to him, "Sir, you're bright and capable—the best officer I've served under. But I gotta ask you, if you don't mind, and no offense, but what the hell are you doing in the Army?"

He did not answer right away. *Now I've stepped in it,* I thought.

Finally he said, "I'm beginning to wonder myself."

"What would you do if you got out?"

"I haven't thought that far," he said. A sober look dropped over his face and I changed the subject.

I took a picture of him on the basketball court jumping to defend against a shot, his compact body surprisingly high and graceful in the air. This is the image I carry of him today, lifted above the earth and stretching for something higher and finer beyond the Army. After Vietnam I never saw him again.

Captain Joseph DeFrancisco remained in the Army and retired a Lieutenant General—that's with three stars.

214

Yossarian

A few weeks after the arrival of Captain Joe, a new fire direction officer showed up. Bob Christenson was a first lieutenant, an OCS graduate and fresh out of artillery instruction at Ft. Sill. I had seen how officer candidates were trained at Ft. Sill. In my Artillery Combat Leadership program I took the same classes from the same instructors in the same building. I watched the officer candidates dragging into class bleary-eyed after a night of cleaning crevices with toothpicks, or scrambling under bunks looking for the contents of overturned footlockers. Besides artillery classes, they had added instruction in military deportment and etiquette becoming an officer. My classmates, without the benefit of this extra training, routinely outscored the officer candidates on exams. The new officers arrived in Vietnam not knowing much, like all of us, but now were in charge of a platoon. They had the impossible job of leading veterans while maintaining the fiction of being in control. Some made fools of themselves; the smart ones took the time to learn.

From the beginning I liked this new lieutenant with his Botticelli face and Tom Sawyer smile. Unlike the other officers, he hung out with the enlisted men and genuinely enjoyed our company. A frat brother as much as an officer, he was a regular at our evening hooch parties, where I once took a picture of him posing for the camera with a sunflower growing out of his crotch. When things got hot he sailed above it all with breezy indifference.

> *Our new fire direction officer went through his first mortar attack this week. He did real well, much better than I did back in May. He's a pretty loose guy. Says his idol is Yossarian.*

Yossarian stuck as a nickname, after the main character in the novel *Catch-22*. At first we did not see much of him. One afternoon I walked into the back room attached to the FDC bunker where the officer in charge slept and knew why. Yossarian had been busy decorating the walls. On one wall was a caricature of then Vice President Spiro Agnew wearing a hard hat with two American flags sticking from it. On another wall was a perfect rendering of Mr. Zig Zag, the black-bearded figure on roll-your-own cigarette papers and the patron saint of potheads.

At first, Yossarian did not even pretend he was running the operation. He wandered around FDC and spent a great deal of time somewhere else. He listened and asked questions, but mostly he joked and worked at not taking anything seriously. At night when a fire mission came up Yossarian never left his bunk. When the guns were ready to shoot and all we needed was the final command from the fire direction officer, he shouted "Fire" from around the corner.

216

Gradually, almost without our realizing it, Yossarian worked his way into the daily routine. He started taking calls on the radio and eventually could handle an entire fire mission, acting as the communication link between the infantry and FDC. He took on simple map plotting jobs and soon could work up firing data as quickly as anybody. Now when a fire mission came up at night, he was out of his bunk, peering over shoulders, double-checking coordinates and verifying firing data. He became every bit the officer in charge. He and Captain Joe were the best officers I served under in Vietnam.

The Long Shot

Shooting bad data was the worst sin an artillery battery could commit. The story was still alive of a battery in our regiment engaged in a routine mission that ended in the deaths of three civilians. The battery was on a nighttime mission and shooting illumination. The FDC had calculated the spot high in the sky at which the illumination rounds would burst, but failed to take into account where the brass canisters would land after they continued on their trajectory. It was an easy step to forget in the heat of an infantry firefight with the VC. Four canisters tumbled through the roof of a civilian dwelling and killed a mother, father and child. As a consequence the fire direction officer was relieved of field duty, and was punished to driving a jeep for a general in Cam Rahn.

LZ Sherry had the reputation of shooting good data all the time. It was a point of great pride. That all changed in the middle of a quiet night shift. Quiet was a relative term. The firebase was always a noisy place at night. The bangs of howitzers shooting H&I and illumination came every ten minutes. All of the powder charges for this shooting were cut to a low charge one. They became such monotony that we quit noticing. On this night an enormous boom went off, and every head in FDC popped up, as if attached to the same puppet string. It was a howitzer, not a mortar—we knew the difference. We waited. A gunner's voice came over the landline, "Gun 3. FDC, we got a problem."

"We figured. What happened?" the radio operator said.

"We fired a charge seven on H&I." That meant a high explosive round.

"Gimme the data."

"Hold on." There was a long silence as they checked the exact gun settings.

Mike Leino jumped on the map board and waited for the information. He plotted the direction the gun had fired and said, "Straight for Phan Thiet," a city of 100,000 people only five miles away and well within howitzer range. The elevation of the gun would tell us how far the shell traveled and whether we had bombarded downtown Phan Thiet. Yossarian grabbed the range chart.

Captain Joe had heard the shot and by this time was in FDC. "What's going on?" he said.

Without looking up from the chart, Yossarian said, "Gun 3 just fired a charge seven HE straight at Phan Thiet."

"Oh my God."

Yossarian raised his head. "It went clear over downtown. Landed a click into the harbor."

"What about fishing boats?" the captain said.

Yossarian stood up from the map table and tossed the range chart. "There probably aren't many out that far this time of night. Let's hope."

We reported the incident to battalion in the morning and

never heard another word about it. In our imaginations the round whizzed over the city, raising the eyes of nighttime revelers, and landed in an empty stretch of the South China Sea.

Buried Treasure

We were never not preparing for an inspection. They came at the relentless pace of two a month. For some inspections experienced artillerymen ran us through mock fire missions and insisted on procedural details we had long ago judged a waste of time. On other inspections men in combat fatigues with sharp creases walked around with clipboards making checkmarks and peering into stacks of paperwork. After one of these inspections a negative report came back citing us for not having anti-ice screens on the radio handsets.

I burst into Top's hooch waving the report. "Have you seen this? Are these people crazy? They can't be serious. Ice screens in Vietnam? What in the world is the matter with—"

Top cut me off with the look of a three-war veteran. "Yes, I've seen it. Yes, they're crazy. Put the screens on order. As long as they're on order they won't bother us. Now get out."

I found the part in the manual and wrote up an order for the small screens. They clipped onto the radio handsets so they would not gather frost from the operator's breath when temperatures dropped below freezing. The lowest temperature I

221

ever recorded in the chill of night during monsoon season was eighty degrees.

There was one special inspection we called the monster. A team would arrive to verify equipment inventories out of a thick binder of authorized material for our battery. The binder included items as large as a 2½-ton truck and as small as a spoon. This inspection would cover all of it. We were to possess only authorized equipment, nothing less and certainly nothing more. This inspection would be our yearly physical, probing every orifice and private crevice.

There was going to be a problem. Junk Daddy had secured for us a mountain of extra truck parts, tools and generators. If the inspection team uncovered them, there would be a messy and embarrassing investigation. There was too much extra equipment to smuggle out, so we did the only thing left to us. We buried it.

Junk Daddy sent the bulldozer 100 yards outside the wire to the northeast, in the opposite direction from the helipad. Within the hour it dug an enormous trench, into which went everything but the enormous Air Force generator. Junk Daddy said not to worry about that. We soaked the hammers, shovels, screwdrivers, pliers and wrenches in motor oil and then wrapped them in canvas. The truck parts and small generators we wrapped in large plastic sheets and then in another layer of canvas. Once everything was in the ditch the bulldozer pushed the dirt over, leaving only an innocent mound. The troops knew the rest of the drill. Everyone wore hats, shirts, long pants and polished boots. Hair was shorn, hooches were free of roof-grass, and operational manuals no one ever used were on display.

Three helicopters delivered the inspectors. There were twenty of them—pasty white and dripping perspiration. To our

222

surprise they were all lawyers and office staff from the Judge Advocate General's office, the official legal branch of the Army. The lead inspector was a tall, round colonel. He chomped on a cigar that never left his mouth. Beside him walked his aide, a diminutive major who looked all the smaller beside the colonel's rotundity. The other inspectors filed off their helicopters, all wearing identical .45 pistols strapped to their hips, as if they had picked them up from central casting for their big performance in the field. The little major wore his in a shoulder holster, bringing it to the same height as his colonel's pistol.

While the inspectors made their introductions and began the work of checking boxes on their clipboards, the major went on a self-guided tour of a howitzer emplacement. He walked around the gun without comment, and to his credit without touching anything. When he got to the front of the gun he turned toward the berm and walked out to an aiming stake. He then bent down and tried to look through the small lens in the stake. The gun crew had been watching the major, and when they saw him bend over at the aiming stake they started to laugh. The crew chief walked out and said to the major, "Sir, if you would come with me back to the howitzer I'll show you how this works. We use this stake to get the right direction when we shoot. We look *at* it, not through it."

"Of course, Sergeant," he said, "but I believe I need to find the colonel. Thank you anyway." As the major walked away he said to himself, but loud enough for the sergeant to hear, "Fascinating."

Midway through the visit, when the inspectors were deep into our records, reconciling inventory manifests and sampling maintenance logs for irregularities, the siren went off for a fire mission. The gun crews swarmed out of their hooches in steel

223

pot helmets and ran to their guns. Others sprinted across the compound to their stations.

The inspectors thought we were under attack. They dove under tables, rolled beneath the nearest truck and ran into hooch openings. Clouds of paper flew into the air. Luckily no one thought to draw his pistol. The colonel crawled to a small fighting bunker on the berm. The top half of him went in, but at the hips he stuck fast. The soldier who saw him said later the colonel made a second effort with a loud "oomph."

When the excitement died down the lawyers emerged from their hiding places, and once their papers were straightened, picked up the inspection where they had left off. The colonel, now unstuck, strode up and down the center of the compound. He worked at the cigar in his mouth with added fury, perhaps to restore his dignity and prove he had not been a bit frightened.

The formal portion of the inspection completed, the colonel called the officers and sergeants to gather outside Top's hooch. He wanted his team to give us their preliminary findings. The first inspector to speak was a young lieutenant. He was concerned about the perimeter defense at LZ Sherry, among the best-fortified firebases in Vietnam. He said to Captain Joe, "If the three towers get knocked out, you lose your M60 machine guns, the two quad-50s, the two forty millimeter cannons, and all six guns—you'd really be in a bind." He was showing off for the colonel.

Captain Joe chose not to mention that we had four guard towers and only five howitzers. Instead the captain laughed and said, "You're damn right we would."

The lieutenant had nothing more to say, and settled back

with a little smile.

The major cleared his throat. "Let me summarize a few items associated with our inspection before we depart. I believe I speak for the entire team when I say how impressed we have been with your firebase here. Especially your performance in connection with the action at hand this morning. Excellent. Fascinating really."

The colonel turned his head to the major, as if to say, *Get on with it.*

"You will receive our full report in several weeks once it has been cleared and properly classified by the Judge Advocate General's regimental review committee. Depending on the level of classification, you have a duty to protect…"

Now the colonel cleared his throat.

The major continued, "Yes, let me proceed to the two action items emanating from our findings and comprising the final section of the full report. While I will use language consistent with these being recommendations, you may take them as directives for your purposes, as the Judge Advocate General's final report will…"

The colonel broke in, "Major, if you will."

"Yes, first we recommend six additional fighting bunkers be built into the berm to strengthen perimeter defense."

We already had plenty of fighting bunkers. If we had needed more we would have built them.

"Second, we strongly recommend that you, and here I believe I can say you *must*, comply with the Army requirement that all buildings display exit diagrams in case of fire. Any structure of any size that functions as a residence or place of work must display said diagram."

The helicopters were barely out of sight when two trucks

carrying men with shovels drove out the gate and began the task of disinterring our extra equipment. By nightfall the extra hammers, generators and carburetors were back in service. The Air Force generator had passed through the inspection without a comment. Junk Daddy had seen that the right serial numbers were on the right lists in the bowels of regimental records.

Before the final inspection report could arrive, we threw up the extra perimeter bunkers in a couple days and began work on the exit diagrams. It was easier to comply than fight, and we did not want any more attention from the JAG office.

My hooch was built for one person. With two bunks squeezed into it there was hardly enough room to stand and put on a pair of pants. It clearly needed an exit diagram. Suspecting that no one back home would believe this piece of military idiocy, I took a picture of the diagram. It was labeled FIRE PLAN and showed two bunks with the words SLEEPING AREA. Red arrows led from each bunk out the door. Where to post the diagram? It was too dark inside my hooch to read, so I nailed the diagram on the outside wall. The confused soldier who needed help getting out of my hooch already had to be outside in order to learn how to get outside. It was perfect.

Sitting Ducks

From a guard tower I could see the base camp of the combat engineers at the foot of Titty mountain to our north. More than once I watched them get clobbered by rocket and mortar attacks. The engineers built roads, bridges and airstrips, usually in remote areas. Their compound was just a cluster of tents and scattered equipment. I thought, *Tents, for God sake, in the middle of a combat zone.* Instead of blowing up the roads, the VC decided to blow up the engineers who built them.

> Perhaps you have been hearing in the news about the retaliation the VC launched for U.S. raids to free prisoners. In this area they really raised hell for a few days. Hardest hit was an engineer compound to our north. Two were killed and 15 wounded. They were hit three nights in a row, but not so severely as the

227

first night.

Causing all the trouble are two hardcore Viet Cong battalions, which are still in the area. Yesterday they shot down two helicopters. We know their main aim is to harass the engineers who are currently engaged in road building. It isn't likely that they will initiate contact with U.S. artillery or infantry.

With every attack on the engineers I thought back to the day I enlisted and checked the Combat Engineer box on the form without half a thought. At night when I watched the distant flashes of mortars and streaks of tracers going into the engineer compound, I felt grateful for finding my way to the artillery. I liked being able to shoot back.

Tube Ring

Lieutenant Dan wandered into LZ Sherry as a lamb among wolves. His first assignment was as officer in charge of the howitzer crews. The lieutenant seemed to have learned nothing in artillery training and was slow to learn the ways of Vietnam. Yet he freely issued directives on such details as gun maintenance and crew rotation, and the veterans soon viewed him as a fool. Were this his only flaw, Lieutenant Dan would eventually have grown into the job, like most new officers. However he suffered from another defect that would be his undoing. He was gullible.

Late one night during a quiet period, a call came into FDC over the landline. "FDC...Gun 2." It was Swede.

"Yeah," I said.

"We have to take Gun 2 down."

"OK. What's going on?"

"Tube ring."

"Say again?"

"The lieutenant's here and we thought we ought to bring it to his attention. The tube ring doesn't sound right."

There were a lot of things to worry about regarding the howitzer barrel, but tube ring was not one of them.

"Put the lieutenant on." I was never sure what Swede was up to.

I said to Lieutenant Dan, "Sir, I understand there is a problem on Gun 2."

"The tube ring, it doesn't sound exactly right to me."

"Yes, sir."

"The gun corporal called me over, you call him Sweden I think, well anyway he had me listen as he tested the tube and I agree the ring is off."

"Sir, which test did he do?"

"Gee, I didn't think there was more than one. He did the one where you hit the tube and listen."

"I see, sir."

"And it was off."

"I understand, sir. What would you like to do?"

"It's bad enough I think we should take the gun down for the night. Check it out in the morning."

"Yes, sir. To be clear, at your direction I am taking Gun 2 out of service for the night." I did not want any doubts about who made the decision.

"Good, I think it's best." He sounded relieved.

At first light I hunted up Swede. When he saw me coming he flashed his rabbit smile. I gave him a look and said, "Tube ring?"

"Sure," he said, producing from his pocket a small brass hammer. He walked over to the tube, placed his ear to the surface and gave it a ping. He held the hammer delicately between his thumb and forefinger. In his enormous fingers it looked like a toy.

230

"And last night?" I asked.

"The lieutenant had his ear up against the tube for five minutes while I tapped away. I took him over to Gun 4 to listen, and then on over to Gun 5 so he could compare. 'Can you hear it now, sir?' I kept asking him."

"What was he supposed to hear beside you banging on the gun?"

"I don't know, but before long he could hear it."

"You know, Swede, I really took your gun out of service. Had to. You're lucky we didn't get a mission down last night. Yossarian thinks it's hilarious but we have to clear the paperwork. I'm calling it maintenance."

The word spread and with it tube ring disease. Two nights later it was Gun 4, and the next night Gun 5, making BULL-WINKLE the latest victim of the epidemic. At morning formation Top said, "Leave the lieutenant alone." Everyone knew what he meant. "Are we clear on that?"

Once the lieutenant learned he had been made a fool, he came down hard on the gun crews. He called for useless maintenance. He made detailed inspections of equipment he did not understand. The crews grumbled but took it. The lieutenant then took his vengeance one step too far. He made every crewman wear hats and shirts during the day, an insult to their dignity and a public embarrassment. Night had just fallen when inside the FDC bunker we heard an explosion, too small for a mortar or howitzer.

Curly got on the landline running to the guns and guard towers, "You guys know what that pop was?"

"Tower 2. It wasn't incoming."

"Gun 5 here. Don't know, but someone saw a flash over by Gun 4."

Curly raised his voice into the handset. "Gun 4. What are you guys doing over there?" There was silence and Curly yelled, "Gun 4, answer."

"Maybe Gun 4 is on R&R," an anonymous voice said.

"This is Gun 4. Top just got here." The voice lowered. "And he is hoppin' mad. It was a grenade. Somebody fragged the lieutenant's hooch."

"Anybody hurt?" Curly asked. "We need a dust-off?"

"No. It hit outside on the corner."

"Who did it?"

"Don't know. Gotta go."

At formation the next morning Top was the angriest I had ever seen him. "Come to attention. You're going to hear what I got to say. In case you don't know, some piece of shit threw a grenade last night. It's lucky nobody got hurt. Whoever did this could have hurt a lot of innocent people. Some poor fuck just walking by all of a sudden's got a face full of shrapnel." Top made no mention of the lieutenant. "Whoever did this, I will have your balls, your dick and your ass in a meat grinder when I find you. I know I'm looking at you right now out there. I'll tell you to your face, you are a fuckin' coward. In the middle of the night popping a fragmentation in the middle of my firebase, my gun crews. I'm going to find you. Any of you get the idea this is cute or it'll make you a hero—I will shoot you myself I catch the next guy that pulls this." Top walked away without dismissing the formation.

The perpetrator was never found. Nobody looked that hard, including Top. An uneasy quiet settled on the battery. Captain Joe took the lieutenant off the guns, which left him without a job. Lieutenant Dan spent his days drifting from place to place, a manufactured smile on his face. He avoided

232

the gun crews entirely. He came into the FDC bunker every day and attached himself to Yossarian. The two of them came to our little hooch parties at night, where Yossarian was the comic center of attention and Lieutenant Dan was happy to sit and be one of the guys.

Lieutenant Dan never recovered. Lt. Les Cramblet, who arrived at LZ Sherry toward the end of my tour, and Bob "Yossarian" Christenson wrote to me about their memories of him.

Les Cramblet:

Our new CO placed him on indefinite night duty, but after a few days he was removed from that duty, ostensibly because he had trouble coping with the night duty hours, and I replaced him. I was told of his earlier problems in the battery, but was not aware of the fragging incident. I was never sure what his duties were; he was sort of a mystery to me.

Bob Christenson:

I recall someone fragging some worthless lieutenant who was using my hooch while I was on R and R. I came back and there was a big hole in the side, and someone tried to tell me that it had been hit by a rocket or some other BS. I think the Army sent him home for his own good.

A Day at the Zoo

LZ Sherry was home to a menagerie of animals beyond the donkeys running the place. My first encounter with the local wildlife came on my second night in the firebase. I was in my hooch about to fall asleep, and wearing only boxer shorts. As I began to drift off an enormous rat ran across my chest. I felt its claws with every step it took from my right shoulder down to my left hip.

The rats were everywhere at LZ Sherry, brought there by the South Vietnamese troops camped inside the perimeter. The ARVN took an army of rats with them wherever they went. And where there were rats, there were snakes. They hid in cool corners and lived in dark crevices under hooches. We were told to be on the alert for a short, gray snake called the two-stepper, so venomous its victim died within seconds. We never saw one and began to suspect they did not exist, except to frighten Americans.

When the ARVNs left a few weeks into my tour, they took most of the rats and snakes with them. One snake stayed and took up residence under the hooch next to mine. He was seven feet long and had alternating bands of black and yellow. We had no idea if he was poisonous, but he was clearly not a two-stepper. We made him a mascot for our end of the battery. Max proved a good neighbor. He controlled the rat population and was smart enough to avoid humans.

We did not adopt every animal in the firebase.

My hooch-mate tells me I've got to mention Godzilla, an eight-inch lizard we ran into while tearing down a hooch this morning. It was Leino vs. Godzilla. Leino won because he had the axe.

Our biggest worry was scorpions. The brown ones, unlike their black cousins, were aggressive and packed potent venom. Scorpions hid in empty boots, in the folds of clothing and under sandbags. We were always careful to bang out our boots and shake our clothes before putting them on.

During a quiet night shift when four of us were playing bridge, I saw a scorpion climbing up Yossarian's sleeve. He felt something and looked down. Normally phlegmatic by nature, Yossarian leapt to his feet, flailing his arms and scattering cards in the air. We watched him dance around the map tables. When he sat back down his partner said, "It was only a black one. Your bid."

Insects were the real rulers of the country. Sharing space with the scorpions under sandbags was a small, ferocious red ant. I discovered them when I took hold of the end of a sandbag and felt my arm on fire. In half a breath they had eaten their way up to my elbow. Their docile cousins, the black ants, preferred the indoors and found their way to every scrap of food in the compound, especially the sugar. After a while I just thought of them as a menu item. It was hard to find an apple that a wasp had not already made her home. Flies dotted the walls and harassed plates of food.

The king of insects was the mosquito. They were thick in the air during the monsoon season when it rained almost every night. They thrived in the surrounding rice paddies and bred in the puddles that covered the compound. In a letter home to my little sister Jayne I exaggerated, but not much.

> The mosquitoes are sure getting big. They eat birds for breakfast and dogs for supper. When one stings you at night he leaves a blood donor card. A mosquito bumped into my hooch yesterday and knocked down three sandbags. The next one I kill, I am going to mount his head on the wall.

I had the kind of skin that attracted mosquitoes from miles around. My best friend during monsoon was Army issue, military grade repellent, 100% DEET. It came in a squirt bottle the size of a cigarette pack, which the infantry strapped to their helmets and I carried in a pocket. I smeared the oily stuff all over my body when the sun began to set. For insurance I slept with mosquito netting over my bunk and tucked securely around me. Some mornings I could see mosquitoes sitting on the netting waiting for me to emerge.

Besides their nuisance value, mosquitoes brought malaria. Every Tuesday Doc went around with a checklist giving out malaria pills. The pill gave some guys diarrhea. Within the hour they were sprinting for the latrine. If there was a line they held their stomachs and screamed at the guys inside.

At the top of the food chain were the big jungle cats. The Le Hong Fong forest and its resident predators were barely a mile away. At LZ Betty a large tiger had wandered into the wire and died when it tripped a claymore mine. Soldiers posed for pictures over its body with their rifles, pretending they had bagged the animal themselves. At LZ Sherry we had our own big cat.

> We now have some wild beast prowling the battery at night. In the states it is called a puma.

Tower guards and gun crewmen reported seeing it around the mess hall several nights running. Then it had the good sense to stay away. Somebody would have shot it before long.

Max, our resident snake, was not so fortunate. A soldier who had been in the battery for only a few weeks walked proudly into the center of the compound holding aloft the dead Max. He held the snake in the air with his arm fully extended, and even then Max's tail just barely cleared the ground. Everybody groaned at the sight. The one wild inhabitant that lived in harmony with us was dead from a stupid kid with a gun. Some of us wanted to bury the kid with his victim.

The big cat roaming the battery was probably a panther, a

237

subspecies of leopard with a black coat. It was no doubt hunting rats around the trash dump outside our perimeter. It would have been easy for the animal to leap the wire in the dark of night and go largely unseen around the compound.

"The leopard is the most successful of all the big cats. There are ten times more of them than lions, tigers and cheetahs combined; and they have spread over half the globe. The leopard owes much of its success to a wary personality and the ability to live with and around humans without attracting attention to itself. Incredibly leopards are known to inhabit big cites across Africa and Asia, living on stray pets, rats and rubbish. They rarely attack humans." (From the PBS *Nature* series, "Revealing the Leopard," aired November 21, 2010)

The Battle of
LZ Sherry

"We will destroy LZ Sherry." That was the quote S2 Intelligence relayed to us from an intercepted enemy communication. A battalion of North Vietnamese Army regulars would attack LZ Sherry in seven days. There was no further information and nothing about the quality of the intelligence. The clerk who relayed the message said, "We just thought you ought to know."

We rarely got intelligence that meant anything to LZ Sherry, and what we did get was so general that it was useless. Instead of trying to figure out the enemy or guess what he was up to, we followed a simple protocol. When he shot at us we shot back. Still this was the most detailed information we had ever gotten from S2. We could not ignore it. We could be facing a combined force like the one that attacked LZ Betty the previous May, a battalion of NVA infantry in consort with several companies of Viet Cong.

By now the drawdown had made a ghost town of the once bustling U.S. compound at Phan Thiet. Even the post office was closed. The ARVN forces had taken over military operations from the 1/50 and 3/506 U.S. Infantry Battalions. All of our fire missions for the past six months had been in support of ARVN infantry. Air support, even for supplies, was virtually nonexistent. In a letter to Kathleen the previous November, I described our situation as "left high and dry." If we had to engage a major enemy force we would be on our own. And we were short on men ourselves. In FDC we were down to just two guys on a shift.

Top called a special formation and when he read the message from S2 he was serious. "That's all we got. The bastards think they're going to destroy us. Men, the NVA are nothing to fuck with. They come at us we better be ready."

The next seven days we checked the claymores and trip flares in the wire, adding a few more of each. The gun platoons cleaned, adjusted and fiddled with their howitzers. The crews on the quad-50s and Dusters, especially critical during a ground attack, gave special attention to ammunition supplies. Maintenance test fired the M60 machine guns in the towers. The firebase echoed with the metallic sounds of guys cleaning their personal weapons.

Everyday at formation Top hammered on the protocol for a ground attack. "A green flare goes up from a guard tower, the fuckers are in the wire at that end. Remember your duty stations, especially you guys assigned to fighting bunkers. Guns, you level your tubes and go beehive. I want ten ready on each piece with charges cut, and I'll be around this afternoon to check. If you see a red flare the little bastards are through the wire."

He paused and shook a finger at the formation, "You guys on guard duty, don't get itchy with the flares. You gotta see something first. I don't want bullets flying around for nothing."

Top canceled the usual guard duty rotation and posted a

list of veterans. He created special quick-reaction teams and assigned them to defensive positions around the perimeter. He said, "We're gonna waste 'em in the wire."

As night fell on the big day a line formed at the latrine, even our bowels were getting ready. I went about with bandoliers of ammunition crisscrossed over my flak jacket. Men wore steel pot helmets and flak jackets even inside their hooches and never let go of their M16s. Nobody slept. Top patrolled the guns talking to the crews and checking again on the beehive. He yelled up at a guard tower, "Put out that cigarette." A guard could normally smoke in the tower if he lit the cigarette below the lip of the sandbags and held it cupped in his hand, but not tonight.

I was not on FDC duty that night. My assignment in a ground attack was to get to the berm on the east perimeter near the Duster and take up a position. I was in a contingent of maintenance guys and a few cooks, among them my friend Cookie. After my brush with him I intended to keep him in front of me in the event of a green flare.

With nothing to do but sit in a hooch and feel the lump in my chest, I wandered in and out of FDC hoping for any scrap of information. I would see Top there sometimes, or Captain Joe. On every visit to FDC all was quiet, even the radios, which on any other night would be alive with chatter from infantry units and sister firebases. The night dripped away, one of the most peaceful in my entire tour. There was no action anywhere in the entire sector around Phan Thiet. When the sun came up I felt the same thing I felt every morning, only this time a little keener. I had survived another night. S2 had no reaction to the lousy intelligence except a shrug from a lieutenant. He said, "Go figure."

241

Top kept us on alert for another week. He said he did not trust S2 to get it perfectly right, or perfectly wrong. An attack could come any night. He continued his warnings at morning formations, but now he began to tell stories of firebases he had seen overrun by the NVA. "I saw three guys blown away with one satchel charge. Somebody shot the fucker but it wasn't me, I was too busy picking shrapnel out of my ass." Top was having fun. Smoke stood off to the side and grinned.

That is when I suspected Top had manufactured the whole thing. I said so to Yossarian. A look of horror came over his face. "Do you think that is the sort of thing your first sergeant would do?"

Everything Has a Bright Side

Monsoon season ended officially in October. But that did not mean the end of downpours.

It's quarter to five in the morning. Typhoon Kate just blew through. It is cold as hell. I'm wrapped in a blanket up to my ankles in water and listening to the tune of water plunking into empty C ration cans. Sure glad I'm not in the infantry.

The Choice

I loved to watch Charlie work. He handled tools and machines with a gentleness that bordered on affection. Every movement was deliberate. He seemed to give great thought to the smallest action. Charlie was one of those creatures who seemed always to move in slow motion, yet accomplished more than two people combined. His eyes were notable not for their color but for the way he looked *into* things, not just *at* them. I imagined him communicating with his gears, valves, bolts and pistons—and they obeying his silent commands. His work had that kind of effortless efficiency.

Charlie was at peace in the company of his machines, and that somehow calmed me when I was with him. He tolerated me with the same patience he gave a fouled spark plug. When I asked, "Is that a generator you're working on?" he tried to hide a smile, but the twitch in his moustache gave him away.

Charlie had come to Vietnam with a friend from his hometown. They were lucky enough to end up in LZ Sherry together and were inseparable. They both started as gun crewmen, and even though Charlie moved to FDC they still lived together in the same two-man hooch. And they had a pact: "here together, home together."

Then came the choice. If a tour in Vietnam ended with less than four months of active duty left, the Army gave an early discharge, called a "drop." Charlie and his friend had five months of active duty left at the end of their tours. The choice was simple. Go home on time and spend five months on active duty, or stay in Vietnam an additional month for a drop and get out of the Army immediately. Charlie was on both sides of the decision a dozen times. He finally opted to stay the extra time in Vietnam, driven by financial worries over his wife and kids. Charlie made $308 a month, counting combat pay and dependent allowances, not enough to support his family. His wife and children had moved in with her mother and were on welfare. Staying in Vietnam an extra month would return Charlie sooner to civilian life and decent pay. Charlie's friend decided to go home and serve his five months.

Charlie said goodbye to his friend on a clear morning. Everyone knew the routine his friend would follow. There would be a short chopper ride to battalion rear at Phan Rang, then a flight on a C-130 to Cam Rahn, that same day if he was lucky. He would fly commercial to Ft. Lewis, Washington on *The Freedom Bird*, the name of every plane carrying troops out of Vietnam. When he landed a banner would greet him: *Welcome home, Soldier. America is proud of you.* There would be a day of paperwork. Finally he would fly home to the real world and loved ones.

Charlie's friend caught the C-130 that evening out of Phan Rang. Two days later we learned that it had flown into the side of a mountain in heavy cloud cover. Pilot error. No survivors. Charlie spent the next four weeks staring into the distance. Again his eyes told the story of his heart. They grew vacant and seemed to look through things, focused perpetually on the backside of the world.

I took a picture of Charlie's friend shortly before his departure. He was sitting under a parachute canopy with a bunch of guys, smiling and holding a can of beer. I never showed the picture to Charlie and I never talked to him about his friend. Nobody did. The instinct for sympathy went dormant in Vietnam. Polite silence was the best we could offer. Charlie seemed to want it that way. He went home to his family as planned. I never spoke to Charlie again and I never heard what became of him, but over the years I have thought about him. Such a knowing soul, wounded by a choice his friend could have made with the flip of a coin.

George Beedy was twenty-one when he died. The casualty report reads:

```
PERSONAL DATA
   Home of Record:      Springfield, Ohio
   Date of Birth:       10/13/1949

MILITARY DATA
   Grade at Loss:       E4
   Rank:                Specialist Four
   MOS:                 13A10 Field Artillery -
                        Basic
   Unit:                B Battery, 5ᵀᴴ BN, 27ᵀᴴ
                        ARTILLERY, 1 FIELD FORCE

CASUALTY DATA
   Casualty Date:       11/29/1970
   Age at Loss:         21
   Remains:             Body recovered
   Location:            Binh Thuan Province,
                        South Vietnam
Type:                   Non-Hostile
Casualty Detail:        Air Loss

ON THE WALL             Panel 06W Line 90
```

Thank You, Captain Crazy

Top stopped me as I walked across the battery. "I remembered you want to be an FO, and were pissed when the captain said no. So I talked to the new BC. He says it's OK if you still want to go." He paused and looked me full in the face. "But I would consider it a personal favor if you didn't." Top had never before talked to me as an equal.

I said, "Top, let me think about it." By then I was starting to look forward to going home and had an early start on a short-timer's attitude about staying behind sandbags as much as possible. I still wanted to tromp around with the infantry and call in the big stuff, but sitting in the dark in my hooch there was a question I could not answer. *Why? And how crazy was I to volunteer in the first place?* The next morning I said to Top, "I'm not going, but thanks for checking, Top."

"Good decision," he said.

Caught in the Middle

A teenage boy came running up to the perimeter begging for help. Viet Cong guerillas had attacked him and a group of other civilians as they rode nearby on their motorbikes. It was common for the VC to attack and slaughter civilians they suspected of collaborating with the enemy, often whole villages: men, women, children, everybody. A light reconnaissance plane was overhead, which belonged to the 183rd Aviation at LZ Betty. We took a lot of fire missions from these pilots, who always went by the handle *Bird Dog*. He verified the story and called for an artillery strike. His aircraft was armed with rockets and machine guns, but this Bird Dog wanted to play with bigger stuff. While we worked up the mission we held the boy out at the wire. His story seemed legitimate, but he could just as well have been a VC pulling off a clever ruse. We could not shoot the mission because there were too many friendlies close by, and in a little while we sent him on his way. We learned later that one civilian had been killed and two wounded. A fourth went missing, probably kidnapped, which was another favorite VC tactic.

Villagers were caught between U.S. and VC forces. If they cooperated with Americans in any way they risked slaughter. At the same time, if U.S. forces found enemy weapons or food supplies in their village, they burned it to the ground.

Happy Holidays

A Huey helicopter sped over the firebase. Something big and green dropped from its door. It landed with a *phoomp*, rolled along the ground and came to rest against a flak wall. It was a Christmas tree, compliments of the U.S. Army. We set the little tree up near the center of the battery. Without any ornaments, we decorated it with dollops of Barbasol shave cream and convinced ourselves it looked like snow.

A cease-fire went into effect at sundown Christmas Eve. The howitzers and machine guns would be silenced for the night, with the exception of illumination. Defensive action was allowed only with a positive enemy sighting. It sounded too much like the conditions at LZ Betty the previous May. Given the record of intelligence reaching LZ Sherry, I was not convinced the VC and NVA had signed onto the deal.

The parties started at nightfall. The lifers were mostly juicers, and congregated with bottles of Johnny Walker and Crown Royal. Their younger counterparts, the heads, gathered in hooches with various agricultural products. A radio operator and I were the only ones on duty in FDC. I was used to the background noise of guns shooting H&I, chatter over the radio and sometimes a GI shooting his M16 off the berm. But now there was an eerie silence, broken only by an occasional pop of an illumination round or the distant sound of laughter.

By midnight it seemed the entire firebase was drunk or high. I convinced myself the enemy could overrun us without breaking a sweat. The VC studied American habits; they watched and waited for the right moment. If there was ever a time to hit Sherry with a ground attack, this was it. I played the attack through in my mind. *Any second now the mortars will start.* The minutes dragged by. *Yep, tonight's the night. They'll be through the wire in under a minute. A Girl Scout troop could take this place tonight.* I was going to be the lone defender of LZ Sherry emptying my last M16 clip and taking a stand with a useless .45 pistol. I was out of my head like everybody else that night, only without any chemical assistance.

A call came in from a guard tower. "I think I hear movement in the wire."

This is it. We're screwed. I got Top on the landline. "Top, we got movement at Tower 3."

"Is it confirmed?" he said. "Ya know we can't shoot at sounds."

"No, Top. He just thought he heard something."

"Call me back when he *sees* sumpin'. I got Mr. Jack Daniels wait'n on me. Ga-bye."

I did not drink or take drugs, but felt way too sober at that moment. I thought, *If this is my last night on earth, I may as well go happy.* I found the hooch where Leino was hosting, and sucked in the warm, sweet air. I said, "Guys, we get hit tonight we're all dead."

Fred was there, another FDC guy who wore a peace medallion with his dog tags and passed dreamy hours with his guitar in a back room of the FDC bunker. He said, "Somebody find this man a drink."

A Falstaff hit my hand. I turned the can over and popped the bottom with a church key to avoid the crud under the lid. It had undoubtedly been sitting in the sun and tasted like wet cardboard. "We're all gonna be dead."

Leino held up a bag. "Let's invite 'em in. There's plenty to go around." The room applauded and guys stamped their feet.

The second Falstaff tasted better than the first. The third was better yet and the fourth was near perfect. After all, it was Christmas.

VIETNAM

1971

U.S. killed reaches 53,849. President Nixon announces, "The end is in sight." Three South Vietnamese divisions, a force of 17,000, attack 22,000 NVA inside Laos in an attempt to sever the Ho Chi Minh trail. They are supported by heavy U.S. artillery and air strikes, along with helicopter lifts. The South Vietnamese allow the NVA to bring in massive reinforcements, swelling their force to 40,000 troops. The South Vietnamese suffer more than 9,000 casualties, over half the original force. More than two thirds of the South Vietnamese Army's armored vehicles are lost. U.S. forces suffer 215 killed and over 700 helicopters either lost or damaged. NVA casualties are estimated at up to 20,000.

The Genuine Articles

Kline came rushing into my hooch with an M16. He had been in FDC only a few months, but had already figured out the angles of life in the field. There was an eager look in his eyes that always made me nervous. "I'm sending this home."

"Kline, you can't send your rifle home. What if you need it for something, like shooting at the VC?"

"It's not mine."

"Then whose is it?"

"Nobody's."

"It belongs to somebody. The Army keeps track, you know."

"No, it's a combat loss. I filled out some paperwork after the last mortar attack and made it a combat loss."

"How'd you do that?"

"I got a form out of FDC. You weren't there. I wrote I was sitting on the shitter when the mortars started coming in, but I didn't say shitter, I said latrine. Then I said I jumped up so fast that my rifle fell down the hole. I wasn't about to go in there and get it, especially with an attack going on. The next day the shit—latrine waste I think I said—got burned, along with the rifle. See? A combat loss."

"Who signed it?"

"I just wrote the captain's name where it said OIC. That means officer in command, doesn't it?"

"No, but close enough."

"Anyway, I made it squiggly."

"You're going to jail."

"They gave me a new M16, so I've got this extra one that nobody knows about. Except now you and Junk."

"Well, you can't send it home."

"I think I can do it. I know guys that have."

"Kline, they X-ray everything that goes out of country."

"That's why I'm going to wrap it in tin foil, to fool the machine. Guys have done it."

"It's still going to look like a rifle."

"Not if I send it home one piece at a time."

"But even if you get it there, a fully automatic is illegal in the states."

"Really? Cool."

"What the hell, give it a try. I'll visit you in Leavenworth."

The next week Fred walked into my hooch. "I want to show you something," he said and handed me a photo album. "I'm gonna send this home to my folks."

"Wonderful," I said flipping through the pages, "I'm sure they'll like it."

"You didn't notice, did you?"

"Notice what?"

"The covers. Do you notice anything now?"

"They seem to be very nice covers."

"They don't look fat to you?"

255

"Well maybe a little, but nothing special."

"Yes," he said and pumped his fist.

"So what's the big deal about the covers?"

"They're stuffed with pot. And you can't tell, can you? Listen, this is the best weed in the world. You can't get stuff like this back in the world. And it's cheap."

"So your folks smoke pot. What is this, an anniversary present?"

When he grinned, his teeth stuck out in six different directions. "No, it's for me...for when I'm back in the world."

"You know if you get caught you'll go to jail."

"No I won't. It's foolproof."

"What the hell, give it a try."

What made me the go-to guy for sending illegal cargo through the U.S. Postal Service? Whatever it was I must have been good at it, because neither one of them got caught. To this day I imagine Kline in his den, a fire going, and mounted above the mantle is a fully automatic M16 rifle, the genuine article from Vietnam. And I picture Fred, seated in a circle of his closest pothead friends, the photo album on his lap, bragging about another genuine article from the war.

When the Military Police failed to show up for either Kline or Fred, I began to think about sending some of my own stuff home that I knew the Army would confiscate when I processed out of country. I had an AK47 banana clip, which I had come across partially sticking out of the ground on one of my jogs around the outside of our berm. Without thinking, I had bent down and pulled it out of the ground. It was only afterwards that it occurred to me what a stupid thing I had done. The VC, knowing the American weakness for souvenirs, often planted articles like this as booby traps. How many training films had I watched about booby traps?

I also had a handful of punji sticks, the sharpened bamboo spikes the VC planted in the ground along probable American patrol routes. I got them from a guy in one of the infantry units we supported. "They're all over the place out there," he said. "Smeared with shit ya' know, so you get infected when you step on one. But don't worry, I wiped these ones off."

I wrapped everything in tin foil and sent the package home to my younger brother Joe. When Joe got the package he was thrilled. A nosy teenager, he gave the banana clip a close look, and then took it apart. Inside, tangled in the spring, were five live rounds. I remember thinking that the clip felt a little heavy, but didn't give it much thought at the time. Then I realized that instead of a few wayward bullets stuck in its innards, the banana clip could have contained an explosive. What a present from Vietnam that would have made when young Joe opened the casing.

Today the bullets and the punji sticks are gone, lost in a move. The banana clip is back in my possession, a souvenir of the things that did not happen in Vietnam.

Irish Twins

My brother Larry and I were born less than a year apart. Our mother summed up our childhood saying, "All you did was fight." We slept in the same bed and battled over covers and real estate, bickering and elbowing and throwing a knee for any advantage. Our parents could not stand the arguing any longer. Dad decided to fix the problem *once and for all*. He built slots into the headboard and footboard of our bed, into which every night he slipped a board that ran down the precise center of the bed. During the day it was stored under the bed. The first night with the board in place we began the evening with our usual battle for the blanket. We yanked it so tight that it popped the board into the air. Larry and I hated that board. It somehow made the bed smaller, and for the poor brother sleeping on the wall side, going to bed was like climbing into a coffin. We promised to be good, if only the board stayed under the bed. But with the board out we never behaved for very long. How often I remember hearing our mother from the living room say to her husband, "Ed, get the board!"

When we were not fighting we were getting into trouble

together with our bows and arrows and our BB guns. Our dad surprised us with the guns for Christmas. Before our horrified mother could object, we were out the door hunting for squirrels and birds. Then Dad moved the family to Kimmswick, a decaying town on the banks of the Mississippi, downstream from St. Louis. It was closer to work for him. There Larry and I took up a huckleberry life, patrolling the woods with our weapons, and throwing small animal cadavers into a quicksand pool down by the river. We fished off a railroad bridge that spanned a creek emptying into the Mississippi, or we stood on the bridge and fired arrows with strings attached, hoping for a lucky shot. It was a narrow, one-track bridge high above the water. There was no place to go if a train came along. We kept an ear out for a distant rumble, or sometimes laid our heads on the track because somebody said you could hear a train from a mile away with your ear on the rail. Years later when we were too big to be whipped, we told our mother and she put her hands over her ears.

Our poor mother. She shudders when she talks of the time in Kimmswick when she was in bed suffering through a late miscarriage. Larry and I were on the bed with her. We had just gotten new pocketknives. One of us—I like to think it was Larry—said, "Let's cut mom open."

After college, Larry battled his way through dental school on loans and grants, which often came through when he was on the verge of dropping out, and an early morning job drawing blood at a hospital. After dental school he enlisted in the Navy, figuring he could pay off his loans and get clinical experience at the same time. When I was in Vietnam filling sandbags, he was in Pensacola filling cavities.

Larry wrote to me that he was getting a discharge. When

he moved his wrist in a certain way, it clicked. Wrist involvement was an occupational impediment for a dentist. The Navy said he could have it operated on by a Navy surgeon, or he could take a discharge. I read the letter half a dozen times in disbelief. *A click in the wrist? Give me a break.* Crazy with envy, I looked for something that would also get me out of the military, something easy and simple, just like Larry.

Guys thrown together for a long time run out of topics to talk about and start giving out details they probably shouldn't. I mentioned in a casual conversation that I could not jump off of anything high because I had varicose veins in my left testicle and it gave me an awful pain.

The other guy said, "You know, man, they should have flunked you on your physical. I know a guy with the same thing and the Army gave him a 4F. Army wouldn't take him."

"They didn't say anything at my physical, and believe me they looked at everything."

"And you think they're the best docs doing those physicals? Or that they give a shit?"

Could it be that this would be my ticket out, my click-in-the-wrist? We had two medics at LZ Sherry: Big Doc and Little Doc. Big Doc was a tall Nordic man with a muscular body and piles of blond hair, a hunk to the girls. Little Doc was short, round, and wore a mousy brown mustache. I hustled over to the medic station and was glad to catch Little Doc, who I thought would be more sympathetic to my plan.

"Doc, I got something to ask you." I laid out my case. "So what do you think?"

"Number one," he said, "keep your pants on, I don't need the evidence. Number two, are you fucking insane?" He started to laugh, and the more he thought about it the more he lost control of himself. He had to hold his stomach with both hands.

I said, "You tell anybody about this and you will have a ball problem a lot worse than mine."

"Don't worry. Doctor-patient confidentiality." And he started to laugh again. "OK, I'll write you an exam order for back in Phan Rang, no problem. But you need a pass from Top and he'll want to know why."

I thought about it for a day. Top and I had a prickly relationship. And there was the affair of my nonspecific urethritis, which Top insisted on calling the Clap. When I maintained it was not, he said my fancy bullshit words still came down to VD. Now I had to explain how I wanted out of the Army because my left testicle had big twisty veins. This was the sort of thing that would set him off, and then the whole firebase would know. I would rather stay in Vietnam.

Alone in my hooch I said out loud, "OK, brother Larry. You win. This time."

Flypaper

The number of forms it took to fight a war! There were forms for truck maintenance, howitzer upkeep, ammunition reserves, personnel levels and fuel supplies. Reporting oil changes on a jeep required a full page of mileage readings, serial numbers and dates. It took more time to complete than a report on a combat fire mission. In the beginning I cared about getting the forms exactly right, checking calculations and writing explanatory comments. Only the daily report on ammunition supplies got a reaction of any kind from headquarters. All the others seemed to melt into oblivion. I began taking a guess at the numbers, and then started making them up entirely so long as they looked believable. Sometimes I put down a wild number, such as having 115 trucks, just to see if anyone would notice or care. Nobody did.

I was sitting at a map table, my left elbow on the table and my head resting on my hand, when I looked up to see a flypaper strip that needed to be replaced. It was furry with fly corpses. Twisted legs and broken wings stuck out all over it. The flies came off the cattle and surrounding rice paddies in plagues.

They crowded inside the FDC bunker and I often found one floating in my coffee. The spiral strips of flypaper, black with cadavers, hung everywhere from the ceiling. It was easy to get one in the face.

Out of boredom I decided the Army needed a flypaper report. I called it the *Flypaper Performance Report* and gave it an official Department of the Army form number: DA 1944A-7. The report contained flypaper installation dates, body counts, replacement schedules, day-to-day comparisons, weekly trends and resupply estimates. I sent the new report to battalion every week with all the other reports.

My fifth flypaper report documented an upward trend in fly body counts. It stressed a need for "increased sanitary measures associated with latrine operations." The latrine was a long wooden platform with round holes, a five-seater. Below each seat was a large metal tub. The flies congregated around the tubs and often made surprise attacks up through the openings. Every day the medics pulled the tubs out with a long metal hook, poured in diesel fuel and dropped in a match. The medics shuffled gingerly around the flaming tubs trying to stay upwind. These were the fires I had seen from the plane over Saigon. It was a devil's barbeque, sending up columns of oily black smoke that clung to skin and made a taste in the mouth. No Vietnam veteran ever forgot the smell.

My flypaper report concluded that waste incineration conducted only once daily was insufficient to control the fly population, and recommended it be increased to twice a day. I took the report over to Doc and asked him what he thought of the recommendation. He studied the paper and without looking up tore it into four pieces. He rolled his eyes up at me and said, "How would you like your right ball to feel like your left?"

263

I never heard a word from battalion headquarters about the flypaper report. In writing these stories I spent two days at the National Archives in College Park, Maryland researching the records of the 5th Battalion. While I verified details of the major events at LZ Sherry, I maintained a thin hope that the S3 Operations quarterly report would contain some reference to the fly problem. It did not.

Redemption

Mail call was a scene out of Hollywood. Guys gathered in a mob while the soldier on the mailbag read the envelopes, called out the names and flipped them in the general direction of "That's me." Hearing my name called was a thrill that increased with time in Vietnam. When the mailbag was empty and it seemed like every name had been called but mine, I felt mighty lonely.

I soon figured out that if I wanted to get letters I first had to write them. On night shifts in FDC I wrote long, chatty letters to everyone I knew, including aunts and uncles I only saw at weddings and funerals. Everyone, God bless them, wrote back. I read every letter six times over, hoping to find something I had missed, a detail or something hidden behind the words. I worked to hear the voice of the person in my head.

A letter came I wish I had saved. It was handwritten. My uncle, a Catholic priest, said he was writing to me, as he was writing to all his relatives and friends, to say that he was an alcoholic. Father Frank was six weeks into a treatment program with the Paraclete Fathers, an order of priests specializing in treating the clergy. Fr. Frank was my father's younger brother. Out of my sixteen uncles and aunts on both sides of the family, Fr. Frank was my runaway favorite. He was a professor at the seminary in St. Louis. Besides a graduate degree in mathematics and a doctorate in canon law, God had blessed him with blue-eyed good looks. I loved Fr. Frank for his irreverent opinions and sly humor. Most of all I admired him for his critical attitude toward the Catholic hierarchy. He and I were sitting alone on a back porch at a family gathering when he said, "The bishops think they *own* the church. Don't they know the *people* are the church?" Fr. Frank believed bishops should serve the people, when all too often he saw they had it backwards.

Fr. Frank had a temper. His students considered him the toughest professor on the faculty for the impatient and sarcastic way he treated them. I never saw this side of the man, but had heard enough stories to know there was something to them.

In his letter to me Fr. Frank owned up to his "defects of character." He wrote that when he said Mass and held the chalice, a representative of Christ, he felt like a hypocrite. He said that over the past six weeks he had learned something new about himself. I expected something profound. Instead he wrote that he had stopped shaving the first day of the program and discovered that his beard grew $1/8^{th}$ of an inch per week. When I saw him next, he said, I would see the result of his stay with the Paracletes.

When Fr. Frank retired from teaching, the college named its library after him. Deep into retirement, when most priests are celebrating Mass at a local nursing home, Fr. Frank volunteered to teach in Kenya, in a little town at the end of a dirt road. There he began a torrid love affair with Africa and its people, so passionate that he wanted to die and be buried there.

Every couple years Fr. Frank made a trip back to St. Louis to visit family and see his doctors, "To get my plumbing checked out," he would say. At the end of his last trip, on his way back to Africa, he collapsed in the St. Louis airport. A smoldering case of prostate cancer had caught up with him. He never made it back to Africa.

Kathleen and I were living in Columbus, Ohio when Fr. Frank was near death. We had time for only one trip to St. Louis, and we decided to see him alive a last time rather than in a casket. We waited outside his room while the attending nurse got him ready to see us, where we heard coughing and tortured hacking for half an hour. When we entered the room Fr. Frank was quiet, the calm that comes from exhaustion. He turned his head and looked at me. His eyes were washed-out gray, not blue anymore. He was barely conscious and seemed not to know me. Finally he said in a whisper, "Eddy."

Later a letter arrived from Africa, from a man Fr. Frank had taught. He wrote that he had planned to pick Fr. Frank up at the airport in Kenya, and had just learned of his death. Fr. Frank had become a father to him as he was growing up. With the letter was a photograph of his child, a son he had named Gaydos.

The Dogs

In the beginning there were three. They had wandered into the firebase one by one, looking for food, and decided to stay. Soon every howitzer platoon and section crew had its own dog, sometimes more than one. Wrinkles, matron of the FDC, did her part by having five puppies beneath the firing officer's bunk. We kept one puppy and adopted the others out around the battery. The dogs became voting members of their human groups, like dogs always do. They learned tricks to earn their keep and went about with their masters like one of the gang.

But dogs will be dogs. They started running in small packs. They established territories and fought over things that only made sense to a dog. One day I watched Wrinkles and her sister playing in the center of the compound. They belonged to different packs but were always friendly with one another. Wrinkles found a crooked little stick, carried it near her sister and started tossing it in the air, as if to say, "Look what I got and you don't." Her sister now wanted that stick in the worst way and was willing to fight for it. The battle ended when Wrinkles got on top. With her fangs bared she forced her sister to a belly-

268

up surrender. Afterwards both dogs wandered off, leaving the stick behind.

The dogs belonging to Gun 4 had a simmering feud going with the Maintenance dogs. The great showdown came when the two packs met outside the FDC bunker and became a tangle of bodies and snapping jaws. The guys from Gun 4 and Maintenance came on the scene and took up sides. More people showed up and joined sides. The men and dogs made a single mob, filling the air with screams, growls and squeals of pain.

Top had been unhappy with the dog situation for some time and this fight ripped it for him. At formation he said, "There's too many dogs in the battery. It's getting to the point where it's not sanitary, with the shit piled everywhere and God knows what they're pissing on. So here it is. Each unit gets one dog. That's it. Guns, you get one dog for all of you, not five. Maintenance, FDC, Mess, Radar, Dusters and quad-50s each get one, that's one for *both* quads and one for *both* Dusters. Pick the dogs you want to keep. The rest go tomorrow."

There was no Humane Society in Vietnam, no doggie adoption agencies. Every unit did its own job. The dogs were coaxed into sandbags and carried squirming to holes outside the compound. M16 bursts went into the bags, making them jump and give off a sharp squeal. When the bags went quiet the dirt went in over them. FDC kept Wrinkles.

An Old Friend Departs

The harmonica and I went back a long way. It was a Hohner Chromonica 260 made in Germany and a real beauty. It was the only musical instrument I ever owned. My parents were great readers, but neither was musical. I cannot remember not knowing how to read, but throughout my childhood could not carry a tune or read a note of music. I always wished I could play something. It was a hole in my life I finally decided to fill when I was a seminarian in the novitiate, a fourteen month program of reflection and meditation. I was never much of a meditator, could not see the point of it, and was going out of my mind with boredom. I hoped that music would be my savior, and I settled on the easiest instrument I could imagine. I asked Father Powers, the novice master, if I could have a harmonica. He took the pipe from his mouth and said, "No. That is not a part of the program." I decided I would make it a part of *my* program. On a rare visit home I went off to the nearest music store. The owner recommended the Hohner and suggested I get the chromatic model with a button on the side for making sharps and flats. I had seen sharps and flats in grade school when the nun drew horizontal lines on the blackboard with an apparatus that held five pieces of chalk. She filled the lines with white dots and then beside some of the dots put tic-tac-toe marks and beside others drew what looked like little golf clubs. "The slide lets you play in any key," the owner of the store said.

I smuggled the harmonica and a how-to book back to the seminary and searched for a secret place to practice. There was an ancient graveyard on the edge of the seminary grounds, at the end of a long grape arbor and tucked into a corner of the surrounding woods. It held the priests and brothers of past generations, their names barely readable on ancient tombstones. After night prayers when the other seminarians were in their rooms meditating, I traveled the dark arbor to the graveyard. I felt my way among the tombstones until I found one I could sit on. I practiced there a few times a week, never hearing a complaint.

In basic training I sometimes played quietly to myself before going to sleep. I played mostly gospel tunes, because they were easy to learn and full of emotion: "Goin' Home" and "Go Tell It On the Mountain" and "Swing Low Sweet Chariot." I played a painful "Nobody Knows The Trouble I Seen." My best song was "Frankie and Johnny." I played it tight, bending the notes till they begged for mercy. In my bunk I went through all the songs I knew by heart, hardly thirty minutes worth, the hole in my soul filled.

One night, just as I stopped playing, a whisper came from the dark, "Don't stop."

And another, "Yeah."

My first living audience. After that I took to playing the same nine songs because I was afraid to try anything new. Every time I played I waited for somebody to want the God-awful

271

noise to stop.

The dust and humidity of Vietnam took its toll on the Hohner. The button to make sharps and flats rusted off. I replaced it with a little wood knob that Junk Daddy found in a drawer somewhere. The internal reeds became pitted, leaving the harmonica without a couple of notes. The slide mechanism corroded and before long the harmonica was unplayable. I packaged it up and sent it to the factory in Germany for an overhaul. I enclosed a letter saying I did not want a new one. I wanted this one repaired because of its sentimental value. Four weeks later a package arrived from the Hohner factory. In it, wrapped in thin wax paper, was a new Chromonica 260. No bill, no letter, not even a packing slip. I raised the harmonica to my lips and blew a single note, rich and alive. I had forgotten the vibrancy of my old Hohner in its youth. I thought, *Goodbye old friend.*

Call in the Navy

For months the infantry had its eye on a VC bunker complex to our northwest. They had observed increased activity around it and now wanted us to soften it up. Here was a chance to use a weapon we had heard about and never used. It was three Gatling guns, each with six rotating barrels, mounted out the side doors of an AC-47 airplane. Together its eighteen barrels fired 100 rounds per second and put a bullet in every two yards of ground. The tracer rounds from its eighteen barrels looked like dragon's breath, and with the roar of the guns reminded troops of *Puff the Magic Dragon*. Captured enemy documents said, "Do not attack the dragon because it would only infuriate the monster." In the entire Vietnam conflict not a single village protected by a *Puff* squadron ever fell to the enemy.

Still nobody thought *Puff* would do any good. Bullets, even a truckload, would never get to people squirreled in bunkers. We called up the mission for the fun of it. We made it a nighttime shoot because we had heard what a spectacular display the avalanche of tracers made in the night sky. At the appointed hour small knots of people gathered around the compound, all staring upward into the dark. The sound of a distant engine grew louder. A flare dropped from the blackness, then another and another, as the plane circled to mark its target. After a brief pause a cascade of fire fell from the darkness, followed by a deep groan from the combined muzzles of the Gatling guns in the distance. The sky went black for a moment, and then another river of red poured down, now from a different part of the sky. In five minutes *Puff* was out of ammo and we heard the engines fade away. Applause broke out in little pockets around the firebase.

We were not surprised at reports the next morning of continued activity around the bunkers. That afternoon we got serious and brought our howitzers to the task. Within fifteen minutes we dropped a couple hundred rounds on top of the complex. The next day activity around the complex had not changed, so we threw another basket of explosives on top of it. Still there were continued reports of activity in and around the area. We needed something heavier than our 105mm peashooters.

News of a Navy cruiser hanging off Phan Thiet in the South China Sea fired our imaginations. It carried eight-inch guns that delivered a 335-pound, ground penetrating shell capable of digging a swimming pool. First we had to fight through layers of Army and Navy protocol to clear the mission. Figuring out how the two military beasts would work together, who would do what to whom, was like trying to get an elephant and a giraffe to mate.

LZ Sherry would direct the mission and an FO team attached to an infantry platoon in the neighborhood of the bunker complex would adjust fire. One radio team would act as go-between, communicating adjustments from the field FO to the

Naval fire direction team. Our radios were not powerful enough to reach the cruiser, so we had to work through a relay patch in Phan Thiet. It got worse. The Army and Navy used different map systems. We had grid maps that divided the country into neat squares roughly sixty miles on a side, good for local tactical operations. The Navy used maps based on global latitude and longitude, more suited for patrolling coastlines and operating across a broad geography. We had to trust that the Navy could convert our grid target location to their maps, but this should not be a problem for a vessel whose mission was inland bombardment.

The day of the mission our FDC was crammed with people, all wanting in on the entertainment. Lieutenant Rudewieck, who loved nothing more than blowing things up, was so excited he walked around on his toes and made a general pest of himself. The others hung around in silence, aware that when a fire mission was underway there was no chitchat in the FDC. Communicating over the radios and getting all the details right were hard enough without help from volunteers.

We gave the Naval FDC the grid coordinates of the target and called for a smoke round. We waited, so long that we began to think they had broken for lunch. We called them back to see if there was a problem and heard they were "still working on it." Finally they came back to us, "Ready with smoke." We gave the "fire" command. Another eternity passed before they said "shot," telling us the round was in the air. We relayed the "shot" information to the FO. A handful of guys left the FDC bunker to watch for the round. A minute turned into two.

We pestered the FO, "Anything yet?"

"Nope. Not a thing."

We went back to the Navy, verified the map coordinates

and called for a repeat smoke round. Another lifetime passed before the "ready" message came and then an eternity before "shot." Again we waited and watched, watched and waited.

To the FO, "Anything?"

"No," he said. "You sure you got the right Navy?"

We had worked too hard on clearing this mission and were not about to give up. We told the Navy that their smoke rounds were so far off that they were out of sight and to please check the data. On the third attempt I went outside with binoculars and scanned the entire circle of the horizon, thinking perhaps the smoke rounds were landing behind us. I saw blue sky and vegetation everywhere, but not a thread of smoke. Whatever the Navy was marking with smoke, it must have been some-where in Cambodia. The next command to the cruiser was, "Cancel mission."

We heard through informal channels that the Navy used this mission as a training exercise for a new batch of sailors. We guessed they were misreading their grid map over a peculiar feature of the map in our sector. The creators of the grid map needed to correct for the curvature of the earth and had chosen our slice of the globe for that purpose. The grid in which the target fell was not a square, but dramatically narrower than the grids in the rest of the world. If the Navy crewmen did not know how to handle this feature, they could have been off by as much as thirty miles.

The infantry never took out the bunker complex that we heard of. Maybe it's still there, a tourist attraction for American veterans willing to fly halfway around the world and pay twenty dollars to visit a site they once risked their lives to obliterate.

276

Big Money

Besides the carnage of war, rapidly rising prices were a silent, relentless burden on ordinary citizens. U.S. dollars were illegal in Vietnam because they devalued the Vietnamese piaster and drove up prices for ordinary citizens even more. A greenback traded for twice the legal exchange rate in piaster; as a result there was a thriving black market for dollars. An enterprising criminal could double his initial investment many times over during a full tour in Vietnam. After his first trip to the black market he sent his ill-gotten piaster to a U.S. bank for conversion to dollars, which back in Vietnam he again converted to piaster. During a tour of duty he could double his money five times, turning $1,000 into $32,000: enough for a boat, a Cadillac and a fancy girlfriend in 1970. But in the process he left $31,000 of laundered U.S. currency in Vietnam. Much of it ended up in the hands of the North Vietnamese, in tight stacks of $100 bills still in their bank wrappers. These bought AK47s, 82mm mortars and M40 rockets to shoot at the Americans. They also bought M16s and M79 grenade launchers, which often showed up in the equipment captured from the

277

VC. I read in *Stars and Stripes*, the military newspaper in Vietnam, of an Army captain arrested in downtown Phan Thiet with a briefcase containing $10,000 in U.S. currency. I thought, *He's buying mortars for the VC. I hope they put him in jail forever.*

Instead of paying soldiers in U.S. dollars, the military issued Military Payment Certificates. MPC came in denominations of five cents to $20. The bills were the size of Monopoly money and had pictures of astronauts and submarines. We called it funny money. Once a month a lieutenant and an aide visited the battery with a briefcase full of MPC. We lined up in alphabetical order, signed vouchers and carried away our month's wages. Most of my pay had already been deposited into a U.S. bank account. I lived on $5 a month for laundry and haircuts, which shot up to $6 when we set up the education fund for Slick and Wan.

On the black market MPC traded on par with the greenback, and helped to further devalue the local currency. So just as a U.S. soldier could not have greenbacks, the Vietnamese were forbidden to hold MPC. The soldier doing business at the bars, shops and brothels of Phan Thiet was supposed to use Vietnamese piaster. However in the heat of barter it was all too easy to pull out MPC bills for an instant discount. Huge amounts of MPC accumulated in the civilian economy, pushing inflation even higher.

Central command tried to put a crimp in the MPC black market by reissuing new bills every so often, making the old ones worthless. Vietnamese were not allowed to exchange the old MPC because they were not supposed to have them in the first place. Conversion day, or C-Day, was a big secret and never announced until the day before. At the first conversion in 1968 over $6,000,000 in old MPC went unconverted, most in the hands of civilians.

"Tomorrow is C-Day," Top said at a special afternoon formation. "That means you turn in all your MPC and you get new ones." A murmur went around. "Quiet. You'll have the same amount of money, it'll just look different. Until then no one comes into the battery and no one leaves…unless you're on a Medevac."

Rumors had been circulating for days about the conversion. A reverse black market was already flourishing. Piaster and greenbacks would now buy deeply discounted MPC from civilians who in a few days would be stuck with worthless paper. The soldier with a stash of piaster or illegal greenbacks could return from the rear with a cache of old MPC just in time for the paymaster to convert them to new MPC.

The rumor of C-Day had leaked days earlier. The nights buzzed with whispers and conspiracies. Requests for emergency trips to Phan Thiet showered the First Sergeant, who was not fooled. It became clear who were doing funny things with funny money. For a week before C-Day, Top sealed the battery so tight the flies needed passes to get in and out. He banned the barber, confined the cooks to the compound, although they rarely left the firebase, and canceled delivery of supplies. If a soldier claimed to be sick, he had to be bleeding from three orifices for Top to let him near a helicopter. Captain Joe instituted the same lockdown for the officers. The paymaster would be on sharp lookout for large conversions. The captain and Top were not about to expose B Battery to a JAG investigation.

Sherry fell silent. No helicopters, no fire missions, no mortar attacks, no radio chatter. It was as if the war held its breath for C-Day. At mid-morning on C-Day a lone Huey arrived with the paymaster, a captain with his sleeves rolled to the elbow. A staff sergeant followed him off the helicopter carrying two briefcases.

We lined up in alphabetical order in front of a folding table outside Top's hooch, like it was a payday. Top stood by the table and watched every enlisted man lay down his stash of small, crumpled pieces of paper. I had about ten dollars. Swede stepped up to the table and poured out a pile of bills from a paper bag. He said, "I think there's close to $1,600 there, sir."

The paymaster looked up at Swede, "And where exactly did you get all this cash, corporal?"

Swede turned to the line behind him and threw out his arms. "I had a terrific month."

The paymaster looked at Top, who nodded his head.

The Old Men

I did not get around much in Vietnam. The few times I got off the firebase it was for quick resupply convoys, one memorable visit to the hospital and two short passes. The only Vietnamese people I came to know well were Mama-san, Cindy, Slick and Wan. They were not dinks to me, but people I came to respect for their hard work and simplicity. The rest I was ready to shoot on suspicion. A three-day pass late in my tour began to soften my views.

I went to the city of Phan Rang yesterday. I wish I had more of a chance to know the people and their culture. Their architecture alone tells you what a highly developed civilization they have. Most of the people are quite poor, but their traditions are strong. I would like to know the old men. They look

at you with authority and they
walk proudly, unlike the elder-
ly in the states. I'm afraid I'll
be shipped home knowing little
more about Vietnam than when
I came.

Six Kinds of Crazy

We were normal guys just trying to get to the next day. Sometimes being a little crazy helped.

At first I turned paranoid about getting killed. I jumped at every little thing, a strange noise or a shadow I didn't expect. I thought—*knew*—I was about to die or get seriously messed up. I didn't know how, but it was going to happen. In that state, at least at LZ Sherry, I could not be trusted with a weapon.

Then I got tired of being scared all the time. So I stopped thinking about dying, and eventually I stopped caring. It was going to be a long year. How long the war lasted did not matter; it was *my* year that counted. I started saying, "It don't mean nothin'," and knew what it meant.

I grew hard inside. Not much bothered me anymore, especially blowing up gooks. I slept through mortar attacks and thought nothing of the occasional sniper round. I noticed a far away look in the eyes of other soldiers, and felt the same look in my own. Yet I would die for the guy in the next hooch, a guy in civilian life I wouldn't waste a good spit on.

I started taking risks, sometimes just for entertainment.

I wanted to be a forward observer during one of the heaviest periods of fighting that year, a couple weeks after our FO team got chewed up at Betty. It was better than being bored. I was a little crazy, but nowhere near the infantryman on bivouac at Sherry who said to me, "I like being right on the edge and seeing how close I can come." He wanted the dangerous missions, loved walking point and had a collection of ears he had sliced from dead VC. But that was not enough. He played a dangerous game with an M79 grenade. The Thumper grenade was designed to arm itself at about thirty yards out of the muzzle once it had spun a set number of times. There was a story about a guy who lay in his bunk tossing a round in the air, like flipping a coin without thinking. The grenade armed and when the soldier dropped it the explosion blew him away. This infantryman got other crazies to play catch with it. Neither knew exactly how many spins it would take to arm. The one who chickened out and refused to take another toss lost the game. The winner got to throw the grenade into the bush and watch it explode.

Late in my tour I became obsessed with how many days I had left in country. With less than 100 days I became a "short timer," a two-digit midget. I took the calendar out of my hooch so I wouldn't think about it so much, which did not help. The calendar had burned into my brain and was at the top of mind every waking minute, along with endless speculation about a possible drop. Short-timers started caring about dying again. One guy wore his flak jacket and steel pot helmet around the clock: at breakfast, in the latrine and even at night in his hooch. "Just in case," he said.

The one-digit midgets could be even worse. I watched a guy refuse to leave his hooch the final week in the field, except to visit the latrine and eat. The whole week he said only one word, "Short." No matter what the conversation or what some-one asked him, "short" was the only word out of his mouth. It was like having a pet bullfrog. He supplied a certain kind of en-tertainment answering loaded questions from his pals. "Dude, how would you describe that thing between your legs?" His answer brought howls of laughter.

When I hit thirty days I quit going on truck convoys to Phan Thiet. I had always enjoyed riding through the open coun-tryside and waving to the kids in the bustling streets. Now the prospect of picking along a mined road through VC infested country, with no air or infantry support, had less appeal. A guy could get hurt out there.

Purple Hearts

My tour in Vietnam ended with a bang. Monsoon had been over for six months and we were deep into the dry season. The well was low and yielded the same green water as when I had arrived at Sherry almost a year before. In the evening the setting sun reflected off the dust in the air and set it ablaze, making every night sky a new conflagration. When the sky cooled to black, a blanket of stars spread from horizon to horizon.

A little before midnight, rockets came screaming toward the firebase. They landed in the wire but still wounded four howitzer crewmen, though not bad enough for a Medevac. Rockets were a weapon more common to the NVA, and that was never a good sign. The VC had grown increasingly active with the departure of U.S. Forces from the region. Now it seemed the NVA were in our sector: a disciplined, well armed and battle-hardened force.

Two nights later I was not on duty, but hanging around FDC. I was now the section chief, after the departure of Jim Jenkins, the slow talking southerner who had originally taken over from Curly. There were a raft of new guys in FDC due to rotations, half of whom I was not sure could handle the technical demands of the job, or be trusted to manage the chaos of shooting fire missions and taking mortar rounds at the same time. They were just too green. Yossarian, Ken Nygaard, and I were the only veterans left. With the NVA in the area, when I was not sleeping I was in the FDC bunker.

With only a few days left on my tour on a quiet night in FDC, I began talking about the things I would have to leave behind. I mentioned that I had two clips of tracer rounds for the .45 pistol. An Irishman named Delaney, new to LZ Sherry but wise to the ways of Vietnam, looked up with a new light in his eyes. He said, "Very cool. You know what we do with those, don't you?"

"Not a clue," I said. "They've been sitting on my shelf for months. Can't even remember how I got them."

"They're hard to get, you know."

"They're not good for anything that I can tell."

"Oh yeah they are. Come on, I'll show you." Delaney slipped into his flack jacket, pulled his M16 from where it was leaning against the wall, threw a bandolier of ammo clips over his shoulder, grabbed his helmet and said, "Let's go." As we were walking out the door he said to the radio operator, "Tell the towers, quads and Dusters we'll be shooting off the berm for the next half hour, direction 3200."

On the way to my hooch to pick up the pistol and tracer clips, Delaney said, "We're gonna shoot 'em out of the air with our M16s."

I knew a .45 round traveled about as fast as you could throw a baseball, but never imagined you could pick one out of the air, like shooting skeet. I said, "Can't be done."

"Yeah it can, I done it before. Wait till you see how big

287

and slow the .45 is, especially at night."

"You saying it's faster during the day?"

He thought about that and said, "Damn straight. Why you think we're doin' it at night?"

We climbed the berm that ran in back of my hooch on the southern perimeter of the battery. From the top of the berm we looked out on a sea of black, serene beneath a canopy of stars. Delaney pulled the charger handle on his M16 and said, "When I tell you, pop one off and make it high enough so it stays in the air. Then watch me nail that sucker."

I fired the .45 and watched the tracer climb a red curve against the sky. Delaney followed it with quick single shots from the M16. The tracer made a beautiful gothic arch and died into the black.

"I think you missed," I said.

"You shot too quick. I wasn't ready."

"I don't think it would have mattered, but OK, I'll count to three."

The second round had barely reached its apex when it exploded in a crazy red geometry. "YES," Delaney screamed. "I'm one for two. Wadda ya think now?"

I handed him the .45, took the M16 and said, "Don't shoot the tracer until I say *pull*."

"What the fuck does *pole* mean?"

"I said *pull*, you idiot. Haven't you ever heard of…forget it. Just do it." I figured there were only a few rounds left in the clip, so I locked a fresh one into the M16 and yanked the charging handle.

I looked up into the sky trying to remember the BB gun exercise from Ft. Sill. Just look and react. *See it, hit it.* I looked high into the sky and said, "Pull." Delaney fired but had aimed

288

low, sending the round on a line drive. I had time to squeeze off only two rounds.

"I think you missed," he said.

"Is that the game you want to play? I can do that too, you know, when it's your turn." I took up my stance again and said, "Pull." This time the tracer went high into the night. I got off maybe eight rounds before the tracer fell untouched to the ground.

Delaney said, "That makes it one to zero, if my math is right. Gimme the rifle."

There were still plenty of rounds in the clip, but Delaney put in a fresh one anyway. He positioned his aim into the sky and said, "Pole." I fired, laughing. He missed and turned to me, "What's so goddamn funny?" He missed again on the next one, which put him in an even darker mood.

On my turn, the tracer reached its apex and was just starting down when it came apart and went off in three directions. I said, "See. You shoot it up right and I'll wipe your butt."

We worked through all the tracers, ending with Delaney scoring three hits to my two. That put him in high spirits as we walked off the berm elbowing each other and arguing about who had really won, seeing as how we both cheated in the beginning. Since this was my first time at the game, I said, "I should get a one stroke handicap, which makes it a tie."

"I don't know what the fuck you're talking about. Seems to me you don't know how to count."

No more than twenty paces off the berm, an explosion erupted behind us and slammed us both to the ground. I felt like an insect squashed by a giant hand. In the time it took to take a breath another explosion flashed in front of us and sent metal whistling through the air. A third cracked further to our front.

The explosions continued, as if the giant were now stomping through the battery. I heard the machine guns open up from the towers, followed by the attack siren calling everybody to combat stations. Now the quad-50 and Duster crews were at their weapons and pouring into the perimeter. We needed to get ourselves to the FDC bunker, but before moving I wanted to hear the howitzers going off. When the big guns went into action the enemy was either taking cover or turning tail, which usually created a lull after the first wave of mortars.

With my face still to the ground I yelled, "OK, Delaney, let's go. We stay here together long enough people are gonna talk." I turned my head in his direction and Delaney was already gone.

Illumination lit the compound as I chased Delaney back to FDC. We had to pass BIRTH CONTROLER, the gun sitting just off the berm, and its deafening muzzle blast. There was no explaining the odd things that went through my mind at such dire moments, but the missing L still bothered me.

I caught up with Delaney at the FDC bunker door just as BAD NEWS, the gun beside FDC, let loose over our heads. The concussive explosion felt like ice picks jabbing into my ears. As we tumbled into the bunker Yossarian looked up and yelled, "Delaney, get on a map. Tower 1 picked up a location."

Kent was on the radios. "Three guys hit on Gun 3."

"How bad?" I asked.

"Don't know."

"Call in a dust-off. Right now."

"Ready," Delaney said. He had the firing data figured for the rocket site. Yossarian pulled Gun 5 off perimeter defense to go after the mortar site. The muzzle blast of Gun 5 was lost in the general mayhem, but when Kent relayed "Shot" from the gun, we knew a little patch of sand a couple hundred yards to our south was about to feel the wrath.

Kent turned from his radios, "Dust-off two minutes out."

"Tell them to hold off for a little until things cool," I said. We still worried about a ground attack and I didn't want a Medevac helicopter on top of it.

"No deal," Kent relayed from the chopper pilot. "He's comin' in hot." Medevac pilots would fly through anything, and this one was no exception. He would barely touch down, holding his rotor at speed while the guys got loaded. "He's comin' in from the north," Kent relayed. "He said just don't shoot'm out of the air."

"OK. Tell Guns 4 and 5, tower 3 and quad 1 to check fire. And tell the dust-off to wait one second or he's going to run into lead."

The ground attack never came and from the aid station in Phan Thiet we learned our guys were going to be OK. In the light of morning we surveyed the damage. We found fins in the berm where Delaney and I had been fooling around. A couple minutes sooner and they would have gotten us. A second mortar hit a shower. The explosion took a bite out of the little box in a perfect semi circle, with radiating shrapnel scars, as if the giant had taken a good chomp. Another mortar hit the ammo bunker on Gun 3 holding around 300 live shells. It hit two feet to the right of the door, went through the outer sand bags and penetrated the inner wall. It did not have enough left by the time it reached the inside of the bunker to detonate the shells. That would have been a real show. The impact of the explosion burned the surface of the sandbags off the wall of the bunker, leaving the fabric hanging in ragged black strips. The wounded were a second lieutenant, a specialist 4 and a private. Mortars did not discriminate by rank.

We learned that an NVA unit had passed through our sector. They probably found a target of opportunity when they saw tracer rounds coming from the berm, a neon sign flashing AIM HERE. Once registered on the first target they only had to add a little to each shot to walk them across the battery. Six mortars fell inside the battery, a lot of explosive for a one-acre compound. We had been worked over by people who knew what they were doing.

The brass showed up on a sunny morning to give out Purple Hearts. Of the several people wounded during my tour, this was the only time I witnessed a Purple Heart ceremony. The first thing the colonel did when he stepped off his chopper was comment on the sorry state of our uniforms. He ordered Yossarian to get us into hats. We assembled in the center of the compound and made our best effort to stand at attention. The colonel put us *at ease* and proceeded to make a little speech. He called the names of the three recipients and directed them to step forward.

In maybe the greatest honor paid me in the military, Top had me read the award citation. Some months earlier I had read a citation for a unit award from the Vietnamese government, the kind of award showered on American units. Intending to make a joke out of it and showing off, I read the script with too much drama. But Top loved the performance and I became the reader at official battery ceremonies. This time I played it straight.

A major carried the three Purple Heart medals on a proper red cushion fringed in gold tassels. Another major—it took a lot of majors for this kind of work—called out the names of each individual from a small notebook. The colonel pinned a medal on the left breast pocket of each soldier, beginning with the second lieutenant. Unlike mortars the military *did* go by rank. Before the last medal stopped swinging on the chest of the private, the colonel and his majors were in full stride for their chopper. Immediately we all went back to work. No slaps on the back, no story-telling, no celebrations. Just another day.

The Warrior Retreats

Top left LZ Sherry shortly before me, meaning we had spent almost our entire tours together. I wrote home about his departure:

> *I will be glad to see him go. I've been under him for ten months now and he is a raving irrational Tazmanian. I have never liked being yelled at and on occasion it took all my composure to ignore him. He knows I ignore him and does not bother me too much.*

Top was retiring from the Army after this tour. Earlier he had stopped me after morning formation and said he noticed all the mail I was getting from colleges. Could he look at the forestry stuff? I had been trying to decide between forestry and psychology as my life's work, not exactly a tight career focus. The two piles of brochures had been growing for some time.

Top said he was thinking about what to do when he got out and forestry seemed interesting. I scooped up the whole pile and walked over to his hooch. He was sitting down. He raised his eyes with a look I had never seen from this veteran of three wars. It was a look of uncertainty. He was about to enter a world more threatening than any Viet Cong sapper, North Korean rifleman or German storm trooper. There was something else he could not hide, envy of my youth and its easy optimism about the future.

We sat and went through the material, talking about the best schools, the ones that gave scholarship money and the nature of the coursework. As we talked I imagined Top going into civilian society with his ham-handed approach to life, a face made old by the sun and a few remaining strands of hair clinging to his skull. Retiring from an unpopular war, he would find few people to value his experience, his skill or his judgment. He would be a holdover from a bygone age, struggling to find a place in a world that had moved on while he was busy fighting its wars.

Top returned the forestry brochures even though I wanted him to keep them. He was not built for the classroom and I believe he knew it. He stood in front of the Huey that would take him away and waved. He held a big smile on his face and pretended to enjoy the moment, a showman to the end.

The closest I got to Top were the games of cribbage we played on night shift and the one conversation we had about his life after the military. I was too much of a twenty-five-year-old snob with a thin skin to let myself know him better. Top had been to hell and back in his military career and he cared passionately about his men. Those were rare qualities in a leader in Vietnam. It is the great irony of my military career that the person I was most happy to be rid of, I would give anything to see today.

I Depart

There were no going away parties. When the days were crossed off the calendar, the short-timer packed a duffle bag and climbed on a Huey. Some like Top got a wave from the troops, but most just got on the helicopter and left, as if on another routine errand to the rear.

> It is the night of March 16, my last night at LZ Sherry. I would like to retire early tonight, but we are having a practice session for a coming inspection. Being the old experienced hand I will have to be there. I start at 6:30 in the morning and usually walk away from FDC around 11:00 at night.

The next morning I packed a duffle bag, exchanged home addresses with a few guys and stepped on the chopper. As we pulled into the air and turned south toward Phan Thiet, I looked for the last time on LZ Sherry. The ground was the same dry-season brown I saw when I arrived. The rice paddies around the firebase showed more craters now, scars I knew would some-day heal. I was less sure of the marks the war had left on me.

What happened at LZ Sherry after my departure I leave to the account of Lieutenant Les Cramblet. He and I have recently taken up a correspondence. He wrote in two emails:

> When I was assigned, Sherry was sold to me as the best firebase and battery in Viet Nam, and I was really impressed when I arrived. However, things quickly took a turn. Top departed very early in my tenure. Top was sorely missed. Top's replacement was an E-7 political appointee from First Field Force HQ in Nha Trang, not experienced running a battery, and prob-ably more importantly, he seemed IQ chal-lenged. He was held in contempt by most of the men, NCOs, and remaining officers. Rather than adapt I think he became more determined to impose his will on the battery.
>
> The new commanding officer (battery com-mander) was also a political appointee from Nha Trang. His previous combat experience was limited to serving as an E-5 FO during an earlier tour. (He) was an OCS product and did not have a degree. He was in some impor-

tant ways seen as less qualified and certainly lacking the experience to make well-grounded decisions. He seemed often uncertain when confronted with the necessity of a quick decision and put off by the advice of subordinates, relying instead on an NCO (1st Sergeant) lacking in credibility. Although the FO experience was valuable it didn't prepare him to manage a battery in the field.

The result was a growing unit disharmony and conflict; in fact, the new Top Sergeant was, in a few months, on the deadly end of a fragging attempt from which he was lucky to have survived and he was immediately sent home on a compassionate reassignment. I think the CO might have felt that he was also at risk of the same fate and didn't appear too unhappy when his tenure was being cut short of the required six months necessary for credit for combat command, due to the battalion standing down.

However briefly, I think in many ways Bob Christenson filled the leadership void after Top departed. I liked Smoke and think he probably complimented your Top Sergeant very well, but I later learned he had some problems within the battery that would have rendered him an ineffective candidate to replace Top in the leadership role he left behind.

Bob and Smoke were largely responsible for my "orientation" to Sherry. They really empha- sized to me that there were divisions of labor and that my role was to largely be responsible for protecting the firebase. However, I found myself in that role frequently in conflict with the new commanding officer and 1st Sergeant. But our conflicts were really only reflective of a larger conflict they had with the entire unit.

Incidentally, during my time at Sherry, I thought of the FDC as our center of gravity, something you should take some pride in for your earlier stewardship and the way you, as far as I can tell, molded it.

The battery moved to Nha Trang in June of 1971 and demobilized in July.

Ralph Part Two

People who went to Vietnam together sometimes came back together. Getting on the C-130 at battalion in Phan Rang was a class reunion of sorts, bringing together guys who had not seen one another for almost a year and who had experienced everything from heavy combat to desk duty. We had no clear idea of who was missing or why. There were only rumors of early returns, wounded or killed.

Yet there was Ralph, the artful dodger at Ft. Sill who had shown me how to take off my training tabs and eat in a real mess hall. He was in a snappy dress uniform that was loaded down with medals and award ribbons. My uniform, that had laid in a crumpled ball for a year at the bottom of my duffle bag, held just three: a Vietnam service ribbon that everybody got for setting foot in the country, a unit citation the Vietnamese government sprinkled on U.S. forces, and my rifle qualifying medal from basic. It was hardly possible to have fewer decorations.

I said to Ralph, "You're going home a hero, looks like."

The old wicked smile came out. "Damn straight. I'm a

paper hero, and proud of it."

"Ralph, I'm just glad you made it out."

"Yeah, right, you too. So let me tell you about this shit on my chest. Every month we got down our allocation of medals. My job was to sort through them and match them up with all the requests. I'd give the ones to the colonel he should sign. You see, every day I gave him a pile of papers to sign having to do with supply, equipment replacement, personnel transfers, things like that. You wouldn't believe the paperwork. Anyway, I stacked the papers so only the signature lines showed and all he had to do was go down and write his name. He hardly ever looked at what he signed. I bet he signed his name a hundred times a day. I mixed the medals in with the other paperwork. I just put myself in for stuff and tried to see how many I could get."

"What's that one with the wings on it?"

He dropped his chin to look and put a finger on it. "That's an air medal."

"But you're artillery."

"Yeah, but I got to know the guys who flew high altitude reconnaissance. They let me tag along when there was an empty seat. I built up my hours in the air to get eligible—that's all it took, just hours with my ass planted in a plane seat. But let me tell you, I only went on the high altitude missions, I ain't stupid. We were so high you could hardly see the ground, but it still counted as a combat zone. When the award got allocated, BINGO."

Still the genius.

Freedom

The plane for home left from Cam Rahn airbase, just as filthy as I remembered it from a year earlier, but now somehow beautiful. As the plane rolled down the runway the cabin filled with happy chatter. When the plane left the ground a cheer went up and seemed to give an extra little lift to the plane. Vietnam was only a few feet below us, but it felt like a thousand miles. I'd never felt that free. Maybe that is why every plane out of Vietnam was called *The Freedom Bird*. It was a good name.

In civilian life the plane was a Pan American charter, with real civilian stewardesses. To my starved eyes they were goddesses. When the plane got to altitude, they deployed down the aisles. One stopped at my seat and said, "Can I get you anything?" I hadn't heard an American female voice for so long, it stunned me. The last time was when a Red Cross girl came into FDC.

I talked to a girl last week. An American! It's only been five months. A couple of Red Cross chics came into our fire direction bunker, and I was in there all alone. I said something real intelligent, like, "Hi."

Now six months later I was paralyzed again. She said, "Well honey, when you decide you just push my button and I'll come." She smiled in a wicked way and went to the next row of seats. I followed her voice down the aisle. "Something to eat? Would you like a blanket?" The only thing I wanted was to listen to her talk—forever. Halfway home over the dark Pacific I turned in my seat and looked to the back of the plane. I saw by the cabin's half-light a boy asleep next to a stewardess, his head resting on her shoulder. I wished with all my heart to be on that shoulder, close to those glorious breasts.

I pulled out a book I had grabbed the morning I left LZ Sherry. Books came donated to Vietnam by the trainload and were piled everywhere in FDC. I picked up *Catch-22* because I wanted to read up on this Yossarian character, a WWII bomber pilot. I opened the book hoping he lived up to my lieutenant who grew sunflowers from his pants.

I read how Yossarian tried desperately to prove he was insane so he would not have to fly more bombing missions. But if he did not want to go on dangerous missions, the military figured it was proof of his sanity, which qualified him for more missions. I read about the general who directed that all tents in the Mediterranean theater of operations be pitched along parallel lines with their entrances facing the Washington Monument halfway around the world. There was the major whose last name was Major. He hated seeing people, so whenever Major Major was in, he was out, and whenever he was out, he was in.

304

I remembered my own "Catch-22s" and the more I read the more painful it became. I thought of the exit diagram for a tiny hooch—if it was on the inside you couldn't read it, and if it was on the outside you didn't need it. The crazy battery commander who parked jeeps facing out for a quick getaway to nowhere, because that's how they did it in Germany. Combat officers not allowed near combat at night. The microphone ice screens we needed to order, but never came because we didn't need them. The ammunition we shot at night because we didn't have it, and if we had it couldn't shoot it. The combat medals for clerks who did paperwork, and paperwork loaded on guys in combat. I had to put the book away. I went back to it a year later and laughed from cover to cover, but on that plane ride it bit too close to the bone.

Instead I turned to thoughts of Kathleen. I had known her now for over a year and a half, but for most of that time only through letters. My style was to save romantic comments for the end, an "oh by the way". From the first letter I sent her from Ft. Sill to the last out of Vietnam, I grew evermore a fool.

I really enjoyed your house party Saturday. A perfect end to what was one of the best Christmases I can remember (excluding the year I got my first dog).

* * * * *

Hi Sweaty - I mean Sweetie,

* * * * *

305

Here is a pat on the butt and a kiss on the nose. That otta hold you.

* * * * *

I can't end my last letter in a minor key. Actually my morale is high, my health is good, and I'm horny as a brass doorknob.

The plane circled over Tacoma, Washington on approach to Ft. Lewis. I felt like an immigrant entering America for the first time. I looked down on rows of houses and marveled at the iridescent green of their lawns. My eyes had grown used to the wash of brown and olive drab at LZ Sherry, and here was a color lit from within, a kind of green fire, making emerald necklaces around the neighborhoods below. On the ground I asked myself, *Were the cars always this big?* Massive galleons of metal, each carrying just one person and sailing politely among each other. How different from the motor scooters, bicycles and rickshaws battling for position in the streets of Phan Thiet.

My first phone call was home and Mom answered. I said, "So what would you think about my coming home?"

Recently I asked her about that call. Mom is now over ninety years old and experiencing the softening effects of dementia, but she has not forgotten the call. She said, "Oh, I remember exactly." She stopped for a moment. "I could hear the smile on your face."

306

Afterword

Just before beginning this memoir my uncle Scott died. He served in Germany during WWII, and after the war went to work for the Army in procurement. Scott complained about the waste he saw every day. At a family gathering when I was still a kid he talked about purchasing helmet straps that no one used. "In fact," he said, "soldiers have orders not to use them. And yet we go on buying them."

I thought, *What's the big deal about a strap?*

But it bothered Uncle Scott to the core. By the time I landed in the Army twenty years later nothing had changed. When we got our gear in basic, the sergeant said to keep the strap on our steel pots buckled up around the helmet. He said, "Unless you want a bullet or piece of shrapnel to take your helmet off with your head in it."

"Then why do we have the straps to begin with, Sergeant?" I was dumb enough to ask.

"To give you something to play with besides your dick."

Scott laughed when I told him the story. We buried him with full military honors at Jefferson Barracks National Cemetery on a bluff overlooking the Mississippi River, south of St. Louis. The cavalcade of cars following the hearse pulled onto the grounds and drove past fields of white headstones arranged in perfect rank and file. We stopped at a small stone chapel, where four honor guards stood at attention, rifles at the ready. A soldier stood on the hillside with a bugle tucked under his elbow. Two soldiers greeted the hearse. One wore the pale blue uniform of the Air Force. The other, a tall African American, wore the striking red, white and blue Marine uniform. When the coffin came into view they draped an American flag over it and escorted it into the chapel.

It was a small chapel. We crowded into the pews. Bishop John Gaydos, a nephew, stood beside the coffin. When the crowd settled he began the prayers for the dead. From outside the chapel there came the sharp report of rifle fire, causing some to flinch in their pews. Then came the opening three notes of taps: the first two quick and low, the third rising slowly and full of pain. The military escorts approached the coffin. They took the flag and prepared it in the precise military ritual of folds, hand-offs and a final tucking of the edge. The Marine held the flag with hands gloved in white. He bent to the family, and said, "On behalf of a grateful nation, for faithful service to his country…"

Most of us by now were wiping our cheeks and dabbing with tissue. The moment overwhelmed me, bearing the accumulated weight of my military experience—the excitement, boredom, fear and anger of those years. Now I felt a rising pride at having played a part in the country's military history. For the first time in forty years I recognized that with my father and uncles before me I had done my poor best to honor our country's fundamental nobility.

In the car on the way home I said to Kathleen, "When I go, that's what I want. The bugler, honor guard, everything. I want people bawling their eyes out." I thought a bit and said, "And see if you can get that Marine back."

Acknowledgments

So many people helped to propel this book on its journey, like an invisible current beneath a frail little boat. I owe a deep debt to four lifelong friends from my seminary days who gave me early encouragement and advice. Tim Coder is a Vietnam vet with a Combat Infantry Badge and Bronze Star. He is the author of the novel, *War Without End, Amen* based on his experiences in the field. Roger Morrissey is also an infantry veteran of Vietnam and author of a series of newspaper articles on his combat experiences. These two war horses and I shared a common experience of combat duty in Vietnam; their suggestions and observations always landed with the thud of truth. John Otterbacher, author of *Sailing Grace,* gave me early writing advice. Ric Miller merits special thanks. Never one to worry about polite language, Ric kicked me out of my lethargy to get serious about writing my Vietnam stories. Ric is a Navy veteran of the Vietnam conflict and inspired me with the story of his own military adventures.

Buddies that were with me at LZ Sherry added context, and in a few cases corrected my faulty memory. Bob Christenson helped me remember details about the characters at the firebase. Les Cramblet wrote me long emails and wove loose ends into themes I would not have discovered on my own. Lynn (Curly) Holzer told me stories of events before my arrival at LZ Sherry and supplied details of our experience together that I had forgotten.

Mike Curtin, retired general editor of the *Columbus Dispatch*, acted as my guide and counselor. He introduced me to Bill Shkurti, author of *Soldiering On In A Dying War* and fellow Vietnam artilleryman. Bill made technical corrections to my recollections and gave me advice on how to make use of the Vietnam records in the National Archives. Mike also opened the door to John Baskin, editor at Orange Frazer Press, who was generous enough to read the entire manuscript of an unknown author and to provide feedback. My sister Mary Kay Gabriel labored through no less than three versions of the book, an extraordinary act of sibling love. Finally I am grateful to my mother, my sister Jayne Nash and to Kathleen, my bride of forty years, for giving back to me the letters I had dashed off as a young man without a thought for the future.

To all, *thank you*.

Photographs

**Myself, in the middle of a long night in
Fire Direction Control**

LZ Sherry, showing the round, sandbag howitzer emplacements
to the right, the dirt berm in the foreground, and in the distance
the creek from which mortar attacks often came

BAD NEWS crew checking the orientation of their howitzer

Lt. Bob "Yossarian" Christenson pointing out the location of LZ Sherry

Little Doc, me and an unfortunate water buffalo

316

Murder Incorporated **quad-50 crew, with killer smiles**

"Fred" and his guitar

Monsoon madness:
a backflip off a jeep into a flooded trash ditch

Me wondering, *will this ever end?*

Mike Leino and his best girl, Wrinkles

**Captain Joe DeFrancisco in a vain but graceful attempt
to block a shot**

Junk Daddy on early morning guard duty

Me and Mike Leino flanking the most important document in the battery, the calendar

Ed Gaydos

Ed Gaydos and his wife of forty years, Kathleen, raised two daughters without major incident and now live in retired bliss in Columbus, Ohio.

CPSIA information can be obtained at www.ICGtesting.com
Printed in the USA
LVOW10s1048230813

349340LV00003B/61/P